AN ILLUSTRATED HISTORY OF
FARM IMPLEMENTS

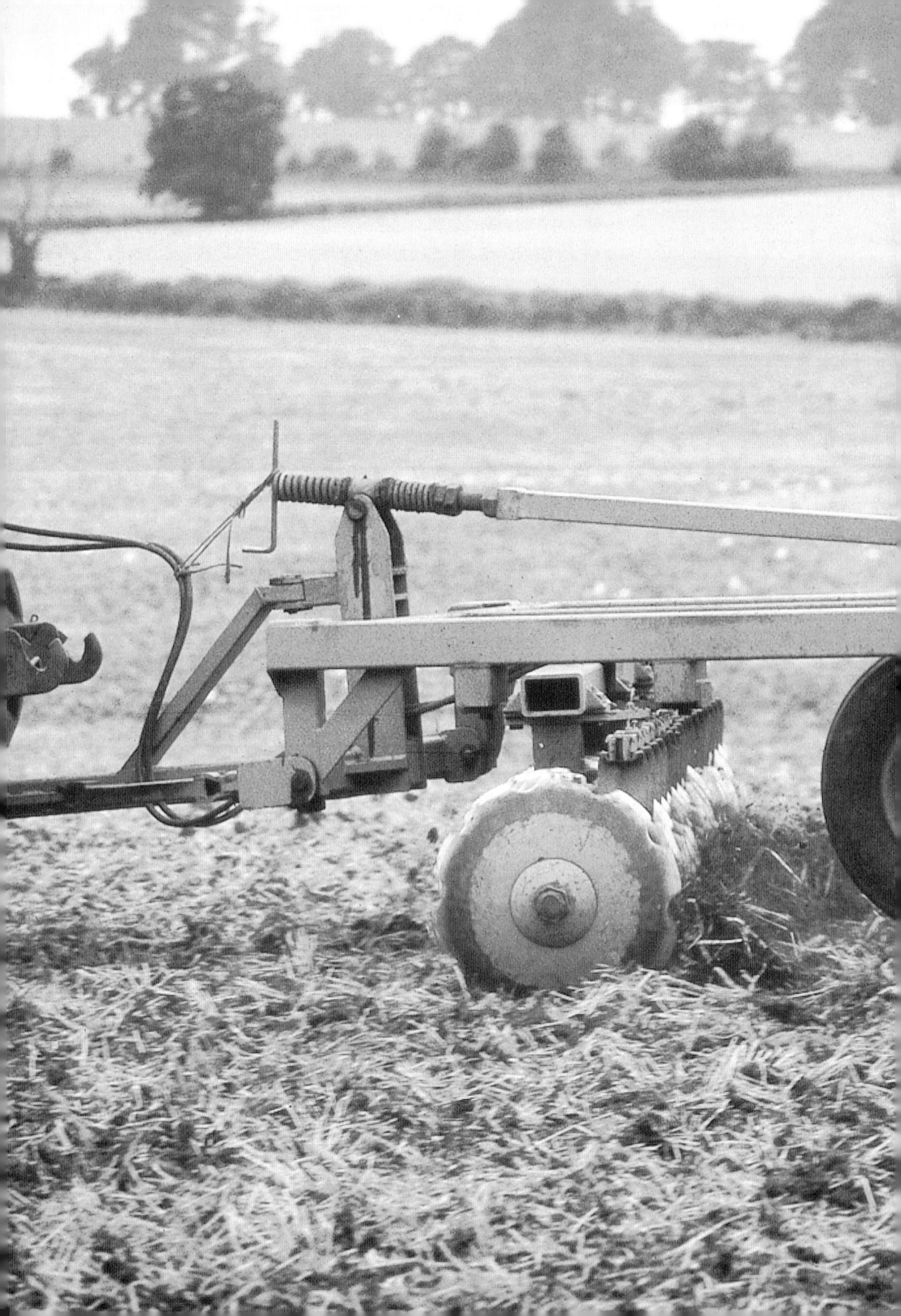

AN ILLUSTRATED HISTORY OF
FARM IMPLEMENTS

Jim Wilkie

Ian Allan
PUBLISHING

Front cover: Ploughing marks the start of the farming year. The massive construction of a modern seven furrow Kevernland reversible plough is a startling contrast to a stick being dragged through the ground yet both were attempting the same task. *Peter Adams*

Back cover: Potatoes need protection against blight and other diseases by regular spraying. Modern sprayers are far more sophisticated than earlier examples pictured and describted.

Title page: Modern disc harrows are sturdy enough to product a tilth even on unploughed stubble. With the wheels lifted clear, more weight is applied to the discs, the scalloped edges of which improve the cutting action through straw.

Half title page: With their New Theme ploughs of the mid-1960s, Ransomes moved from bolted-together construction to a triangular frame of box steel construction. Ransomes' demonstrators were always excellent ploughmen, and you are unlikely to see many straighter furrows than these. By a fortunate choice of location and weather conditions the picture demonstrated that little further cultivation will be needed to get an excellent tilth. *RLM*

PICTURE CREDITS

Unless otherwise credited, all the photographs shown in this book have been taken by the author or are from the author's collection.

ACKNOWLEDGEMENTS

My thanks are due to the many farmers, drivers and operators who have contributed stories, suggestions and recollections. Similar information has come from fellow members of the agricultural machinery trade, and many of the recollections of older members, some no longer with us, stretch back a long way. Much of this information emerged from casual chats rather than formal research.

In the period from the mid-1930s to the 1970s many manufacturers used 16mm film to explain how they felt their equipment should be used. These were supplemented by my accumulation of many old text books and literature. Watching these films and searching through back numbers of magazines have cleared up many mysteries.

Most of the photographs in this book were taken long before the book was planned by the author. If you operate machinery you might even discover after all this time why some strange chap stopped and photographed you from a distance, waved and drove off! Richard Lee Magazines (RLM) publishes the trade magazine *Tractor Trader*, and has allowed us to use some of its archive of manufacturers' publicity shots sent to it over the years. Teagle of Truro provided the illustrations of their hitch.

Much of the older machines have survived only by the efforts of enthusiastic owners to preserve them in a usable condition.

CONTENTS

	Acknowledgements	4
	Introduction	5
1.	Why Farmers Buy Implements	6
2.	Meeting Farmers' Needs: The Evolution of Implements	12
3.	Before Tractors: Horse and Steam	26
4.	Ploughing: The Start of the Farming Year	37
5.	The Three-point Linkage: A Simple Yet Revolutionary Idea	54
6.	Cultivation: Preparing the Soil	64
7.	Sowing the Seed	80
8.	Hoeing, Spraying and Fertilising	91
9.	Transport and Mechanical Handling	106
	Epilogue	127

First published 2002

ISBN 0 7110 2773 0

All rights reserved. No part of this book may be reproduced or transmitted in any form or by any means, electronic or mechanical, including photocopying, recording or by any information storage and retrieval system, without permission from the Publisher in writing.

© Jim Wilkie 2002

Published by Ian Allan Publishing

an imprint of Ian Allan Publishing Ltd, Hersham, Surrey KT12 4RG.

Printed by Ian Allan Printing Ltd, Hersham, Surrey KT12 4RG.

Code: 0202/A3

INTRODUCTION

In what we like to call the 'developed world' today, most people take it for granted that somebody else will produce all the food they intend to eat during their lifetime. Without any thought as to how this will be achieved, they are confident that 'somebody' will ensure that they will never go hungry. In large parts of the world this daily miracle is accomplished.

A farmer's work is never done. To help keep up with this work he started with his own skill and labour. When that was not enough, family help and possibly hired labour got more work done. Even simple hand tools increased the amount that could be achieved. With luck, their combined efforts might produce enough food each year to feed their immediate family. This way of life was just about acceptable if every member of every family was involved in farming.

The first step in increasing output was to 'persuade' wild animals to assist the farmer in his work. Depending on the part of the world, horses, oxen, camels, donkeys and even elephants have been pressed into service. To get useful work out of these domesticated animals, some form of harness or yoke was needed, and attached to this were the first implements. Admittedly, to our eyes these yokes look crude, being little more than a suitably shaped chunk of tree. The hope was that even after feeding the animals there would be extra food that could be sold.

As farms have grown bigger and more 'efficient', fewer people have been needed to work on the land. If you look back into your family's history you are quite likely to find ancestors who started life working on the land but later moved to live in a town. In 1821 roughly 33% of the working population in Britain was still involved in agriculture; 100 years later that figure had fallen to 7%. Over the next 50 years another half-million workers left agriculture. Some moved to seek better wages and conditions. Others were finding that new implements were making their skills and abilities redundant. In many cases the adaptable, hard-working attitude instilled on the farm proved to be an asset in the new urban occupations. Fittingly, many implement-makers preferred to recruit workers with a rural background.

Once a farmer had surplus food to sell or barter, he could afford to pay specialists to do work and supply equipment for the farm. One of these specialists was the implement-maker. In this book we will take a look at the work of the implement-maker and how his products have helped farmers to grow the crops to keep you fed.

To find out more about related subject areas, readers may also be interested in other 'Illustrated History' titles from Ian Allan Publishing which deal with tractors, combine harvesters and forklift trucks.

Below: **During World War 2, with help difficult to find and machinery in short supply, many farmers turned to Land Army girls to help out. With only hand tools and barrows they were often asked to do overwhelming tasks, but mostly they coped.**

1. Why Farmers Buy Implements

Since implements cost money, few farmers will be willing to invest in them unless they feel that they will repay them in the long run. Therefore people trying to sell machinery dress up their appeal in all sorts of ways, but in most cases their messages can be reduced to 'You will get the job done quicker or cheaper', or 'By using this implement your yields will improve, or your costs will fall'.

Over the last few years two other appeals have been added: 'If you are paying someone else to work for you, you want to get the maximum output for the wages you are paying' or 'Since you cannot afford to pay others to do the work, you will find the job more pleasant using this implement'. External pressures mean that even today the farmers of the world find themselves at different stages in this story of development. Farm policy can

Above: There are some implements that an individual farmer cannot buy. The frozen pea business created a need for a specialised harvester, which was usually operated by a frozen pea factory or a producer group with contracts to a specific factory. Mather & Platt specialised in complex food processing machinery, and as a result pea-viners were made by a firm not normally associated with agricultural engineering. Each machine was built to a specific order, and since harvesting had to be synchronised with processing, a mobile pea-viner was more a part of the factory machinery than a farm implement. The factory usually provided the powerful tractor needed to pull the viner, and the farmer was simply informed on what date and at what hour harvesting would commence.

Above left: Sometimes the right decision in farming is to ignore progress and do nothing. While many people flocked to demonstrations of this Ivel 'Agricultural Motor', few placed orders, their argument being that sticking to horses would be better. While the Ivel did what was claimed for it, few users were able to produce convincing figures for savings over its normal working life.

Bottom left: Another concept that took a long time to catch on was the high-speed tractor. This Latil of the 1930s had four-wheel drive, four-wheel steering, sprung suspension, a built-in winch, an option of pneumatic tyres all round, and was fast for its time. However, despite plenty of demonstrations, only timber merchants and industrial users saw its potential. Again, farmers were probably right to feel that it was too advanced for their needs.

be affected by the type of land available for farming, who owns or controls that land, and competition from other suppliers of food.

Implement designers and manufacturers can only supply farmers able to spend money on equipping their farms. This means that individual subsistence farmers still make or modify their own implements. Worthy exceptions are certain charities that are developing and supplying intermediate technology implements of particular use to small farmers. Even something as basic as a well and pump can transform life in a village.

BEFORE WORLD WAR 1

At the beginning of the 20th century farmers had two main sources of power on the land to help them tackle the work: manpower and horses. Labourers accepted low wages, long hours and poor conditions, so farms could employ large numbers of men and some women to get the work done. Where

Above: Drainage is vital to get water away from the land, but no single farmer could achieve this, so low-lying areas are controlled by drainage boards that can justify specialised machinery like this JCB Long Reach, which might put in a brief appearance on a farm. The farmer also benefits from the minimal damage as the machine tackles essential winter maintenance on the Fens near Peterborough.

manpower was not enough, they were assisted by horses trained to pull implements, as well as carts and wagons for transport. Any mechanical assistance would be limited to a visiting steam engine with the threshing set, and perhaps a steam ploughing outfit if the farm was big enough.

Away from the farm changes had come about with the spread of railways, which had made it rather easier to bring in supplies from further away from the farm. Just as important, they had made it easier for farmers to visit other parts of the country and especially major agricultural shows to see progressive ideas of farming from elsewhere. A good and prosperous farmer would be recognised by the quality of the livestock and horses used on his farm.

Changes, however, were afoot. The American prairies were being opened up. Wheat was being produced in large quantities overseas, shipped to England, and distributed by these new railways. This was providing competition to home-grown cereals, and farmers were beginning to find their prices and returns affected by the production of farmers thousands of miles away. Refrigerated ships were beginning to steam from Australia and New Zealand bringing meat to the London markets. Again this offered a cheaper alternative to home production. As a result, British farming found itself in the doldrums: the area of crops grown by cultivation was reducing and the area of grassland was increasing as farm profits were falling.

However, there were developments taking place in certain parts of the country. For example, Dan Albone of Biggleswade, Bedfordshire, previously known as a bicycle manufacturer, had demonstrated his Ivel 'Agricultural Motor.' Once mechanical power was introduced to farms, he claimed that with the right implements a tractor could do the work of many animals, and with no need to grow feed for working animals, more food could be grown for sale. The 'savings' on wages provided much of the justification for buying new equipment.

Farmers buying implements have always been faced with a choice. Alternative designs, types and sizes are offered by different makers, despite being intended to do the same job. As we will discover, there are reasons for these variations.

Many of the first tractor implements to be used were of course based on the design of the horse-drawn equipment currently in use. In time, however, as tractor design developed, more and more implements were specially designed or extensively modified for use with agricultural tractors. In many cases the job they were doing was almost unchanged, but the rate at which they were getting the work done improved.

With prices depressed and natural scepticism about the newfangled internal combustion engine, the spread of tractors was slow, and it took the outbreak of World War 1 in 1914 to improve prices.

WORLD WAR 1

There were two reasons for these improvements in prices. German submarines were attacking ships bringing imported food to Britain, which led to a fear of food shortages. Overseas suppliers realised that they could demand higher prices for shipped foodstuffs. For British farmers offered the equivalent prices, this represented a vast improvement in income. Also, patriotic farmers were anxious to produce as much as possible to feed the country.

The demands of war affected those manufacturing companies that might otherwise have been producing British tractors, but were instead engaged in military work. Most early tractors were therefore imported from the United States, which resulted in the appearance here of some fairly unsuccessful models. Nevertheless, even these could do useful work. Probably the most effective tractors imported were the International Titan and later what was to become the Fordson. Many were operated by the Ministry of Munitions for contract work on farms. Typically this involved work for the British Army, preparing the vast amounts of fodder and forage required to keep its horses supplied, which in many cases had been commandeered from farms, leaving farmers short of power. Farms were also often short of manpower, as the fit young men had volunteered. To achieve the required output, farmers were therefore rather more willing to consider buying a tractor for the first time.

Surprisingly, Lord Northcliffe, publisher of the Daily Mail, became involved in the tractor business, as it was he who persuaded Henry Ford to rush the Fordson tractor into production. Even so, by the end of the war there were still only a few thousand tractors in use on British farms. The vast majority of farmers were still convinced that horsepower could supply their power needs.

THE 1920S AND A FALL IN PROFITS

Following the end of the war many men returned to agriculture after service with mechanised regiments. They were far more familiar with the idea of self-propelled machinery than a few years earlier. Prices also held for a short period after the war. Much more significantly, farmers were promised that they would hold for the foreseeable future. This, they were told, meant that they could invest with confidence. However, these 'guarantees' soon proved worthless, and from the early 1920s prices

Below: Liquid fertilisers were first promoted as labour-saving; instead of a man handling bags of fertiliser, the solutions could be pumped, reducing manual effort. A few years later the appeal changed: by using cut-price ingredients and mixing his own fertiliser, a farmer's costs could be reduced, and the fertiliser could be blended to more closely suit the nutrient needs of a particular field and crop. Before considering the purchase or even the hire of an implement, a farmer first has to think through his approach to getting the work done.

gradually collapsed. Most farmers were more concerned with keeping going than investing in new equipment.

Even so, in many parts of the country there would be at least one or two farms where the farmer was using tractors, and of course his neighbours would be taking an interest in how they were getting on.

Farming was pretty depressed throughout the 1920s, a period culminating in the Wall Street Crash of 1929. The Great Depression meant that the situation got even worse, and the effects lasted for many years. Rather than growing crops to increase profits, farmers were tending to let farms fall into a state of neglect, possibly growing grass, or just letting it tumble down to seed; this was known as 'dog and stick farming'. Livestock numbers were down and stock could be overwintered with the minimum of hay and bought-in food. Only a minimum of manpower needed to be employed. This survival strategy sometimes worked and allowed farmers to keep going until times improved. It also meant that buying new machinery rarely figured in their plans.

Eventually there were some signs that prices might be improving. For example, organisations such as the Milk Marketing Board were established, and farmers supplying them could have a little more confidence in the prices they would be getting for their produce.

War Clouds Loom Again

By 1937 some commentators were foreseeing another war, and planning was started to consider future needs for food. These plans were activated with the outbreak of World War 2 in September 1939. With a huge sense of shock, the country realised once again that submarine action was going to cause food shortages, and imported food could not be relied on.

British farmers were urged to increase production as fast as possible. They were promised excellent prices for anything they could grow, and often they were compelled to grow crops that they would not otherwise have considered. To achieve these objectives tractors were now seen as essential. Farmers bought tractors, and contractors bought tractors to carry out work for farmers who couldn't afford their own. The War Agricultural Executive Committees also bought tractors, and acted as contractors and machinery hirers of last resort. It was imperative that whatever happened, the work must get done. It was no time to worry about whether or not it was actually going to show a profit.

In this situation farmers could see huge potential, and were eager to get hold of any machinery that was available. In practice the most likely tractor they would get was a Fordson produced in vast numbers at Dagenham. If they had a special need they might be permitted an imported American tractor.

Some of these tractors actually came with pneumatic tyres. For the first time it was realistic to think of using a tractor for road work and for transport. To get the most from each tractor, implements were needed; indeed, each tractor would need several implements.

Postwar Recovery

With the war won, it was found that the high cost had depleted Britain's reserves of foreign exchange, and one worthwhile saving was to grow more food at home. Once again guarantees of future prices were given. The currency shortages continued, and despite being naturally cautious most farmers accepted that this time the situation was different and these prices would prevail. Indeed, unlike World War 1, prices did remain firm for several years.

Farmers were therefore able to consider more investment in tractors in the late 1940s and even the early 1950s. Production in Coventry of the little Ferguson tractor started in 1947. Based on the American-built Ford Ferguson, it came with its own range of specialised implements, which could be used only with the tractor, turning it into a small mobile self-propelled specialist machine.

From the late 1950s the era of guaranteed prices came under attack, and so-called efficiency savings were used to justify a gradual reduction in prices. At the same time wages were still rising, and it began to make more economic sense for farmers to think in terms of better machinery and fewer employees. This effectively is what has been happening ever since.

Machines have become more efficient with higher output, and employed labour on farms is still falling. Fewer machines are now working harder and covering a larger area. New safety legislation saw the introduction of safety cabs on new tractors in 1970, and later some form of protection on earlier tractors.

As new and improved machines were being bought, older machinery was being discarded. Much of this was still quite serviceable, and astute smaller farmers realised that a used high-output machine could suit them better than a new machine with a smaller output.

Above: Harvesting some crops is such a quick job that few farms could justify buying the equipment. Even carting the harvested crop is too big a job for most farms. The skill of an agricultural contractor is therefore to find enough work to keep a high-output machine like this Claas Jaguar 820 forager harvester at work. Earlier in the year it would have been cutting grass for silage; now it is harvesting maize for winter feed. When it stops work, the tractors will be out on cultivation work. A contractor's aim is to keep his implements working for as many hours as possible each year, so that he can do some jobs for a farmer more economically than if the farmer bought his own equipment.

Experts such as advisors, lecturers, consultants, accountants and bank managers keep telling such farmers that they are 'over-mechanised'. The big difference is that the 'experts' have nice comfortable offices. The farmer knows that a big old machine will get the job done before the weather deteriorates, and will perhaps give him enough time to get another job done as well. To the casual observer it therefore appears that a particular machine may be used only for a few days each year. It also means that so-called obsolete machinery can still be doing a worthwhile commercial job of work many years after it was manufactured.

These trends have continued over the last 30 years. As farmers have retired or gone out of farming, others have taken on more work. This might have been for neighbours, contract farming or by renting or buying more ground, but they have been trying to increase the size of their operations so that they can justify larger machines to do the work.

Those with long memories will have fond mental pictures of crowded fields at sowing and harvest with several tractors and horses all working in the same field. Now, at the start of the new century, it is much more typical that over even a broad landscape only one big specialised outfit will be seen. High work rates mean that the remaining drivers are able to cultivate a larger area of ground and produce the necessary crops from it.

This pattern is likely to continue, and outfits are getting much more sophisticated. Tractors are now often able to mount various implements at once, allowing several jobs to be done in one pass over the land. Farmers and contractors also operate specialised self-propelled machines capable of doing jobs at a high speed, but they find they need to be used over a large area to be economic.

In subsequent chapters we will be looking at how implements changed over the years. Once power came from one or more horses. Today's implements are operated by turbo-charged monster tractors with four-wheel drive, air-conditioned cabs, built-in computers, radar and computer control, and the driver can keep in touch with world news and market prices from the comfort of his driving seat. Certainly few industries have seen such dramatic changes in the equipment used.

2. Meeting Farmers' Needs: The Evolution of Implements

Before we look at particular implements, let us consider some of the common factors that influence a manufacturer and his designers.

First and foremost, any new implement needs to be an improvement over the present method. Then the manufacturer needs to be able to show customers why and how it is better. Farmers have to be convinced that spending money on this improvement will make their farming easier or more profitable. Having done the job the previous way they are well placed to judge any improvement.

Changes in the design of implements are of three main types. One is gradual evolution, where new or better components are used but the implement still does the job in the same way and, despite the improvements, is still recognisably the same implement. As we will see, a modern plough is very different from a single-furrow horse-plough, while still doing the same job. A particularly good demonstration of varied approaches to solving the same problem can be seen in trailer evolution in late 1940s, described in Chapter 9.

Just occasionally a radical redesign comes along, as in the distribution of fertiliser, where new implements do the same job but in a different way. The spinning-disc fertiliser spreader replaced the fertiliser distributor, then came the wagging spout and the pneumatic spreader.

Sometimes a new technique opens up a market

Left: Plough evolution: this surviving example of an early horse-plough is safely on display at the Yorkshire Farming Museum, and shows how suitably shaped wood made a sturdy frame. The design only needed a basic workshop, and mainly used local materials. Typically it would be built by a local craftsman to suit the needs of the area. While the blacksmith would provide the ironwork, the carpenter would make the wooden parts.

Above right: Ransomes was a major manufacturer of ploughs, and its implements were built up from a number of components bolted together, which meant that individual components could be made in large numbers in the factory and many different types of plough, and other implements, could be built up from a mixture of ready-made parts. It also meant any damaged part could be replaced. This method of construction served the firm well until competitors began to build implements on purpose-built frames, which were stronger.

Bottom right: A modern reversible plough projects for quite a distance behind a powerful tractor, and when turning a corner the driver of this Ford 8670 has to be keenly aware of the length and swing of his five-furrow reversible Dowdeswell Delta Furrow with slatted mouldboards. Dowdeswell made their reputation by building big ploughs to match bigger tractors.

for an entirely new type of implement, as for example in the development of weedkillers. Suddenly farmers needed equipment to apply a diluted spray solution accurately at low application rates, as examined in Chapter 8.

Another influence on implement design is the quantity likely to be made, which will depend not only on the likely demand but also on the size of the manufacturer's business. Ambitious sales targets will mean that even pence saved in design will be well worth while. Take for example the manufacture of a Ferguson implement such as the two-furrow plough, where an extremely cost-effective design could be made because Ferguson

Left: Improvements sometimes result from research. While individual manufacturers can use their resources for specific research projects, the National Institute of Agricultural Engineering (NIAE) is a Government-financed research organisation, undertaking fundamental research as well as more general research aimed at increasing the productivity of machinery. This bridge hitch being demonstrated in 1974 enabled a seed drill to be towed behind a power harrow, and tight turns could be made without the two implements fouling.

Below: The compact Fordson was designed to pull implements, but to mount an implement like this early hedge-trimmer was much more difficult. The front mounting is a saddle fitted around the radiator filler cap, while another saddle is fitted over the transmission with a timber crosspiece butted against the fuel tank. Only with the tractor firmly gripped by this structure was it possible to start adding the main superstructure. A separate engine was needed to provide a continuous power supply, while adjustments were by a winch coupled to the hand wheel. All this represented extra cost for the maker and made it uneconomic for the user to consider transferring the machine to another make of tractor.

knew with reasonable confidence that they were going to make and sell this plough in large quantities. However, a more traditional firm of agricultural engineers, like Fisher Humphries, would expect to make far fewer, with sales targets in the hundreds rather than the tens of thousands, which must have affected their initial design and costing. Yet Ferguson did not have the facilities or the resources to make the ploughs; contractors manufactured all the Ferguson System implements to the company's design, while Ferguson only sold them.

In Grantham, over optimistic predictions were made for the sales of the Kendall tractor, which was to be of a new revolutionary lightweight type.

However, the Kendall's poor design meant that sales were disappointing; no matter how good the hype, farmers soon recognise an unsatisfactory model. Moreover, making implements to suit the Kendall would have proved far less profitable than producing implements for the Ferguson tractor.

If a manufacturer invested in a foundry, castings would be the preferred method of construction. The most surprising components could be built of cast iron: Bamfords of Uttoxeter even fitted a substantial cast-iron toolbox to its mowers, which featured a cup-holder to take the oilcan. So many firms used seats of cast iron that collectors now restore and exhibit them. By contrast, the founder of JF Machinery in Denmark attributed the firm's success to not having a foundry; instead light and strong components were fabricated, and the weight savings made them cheaper to build and lighter to pull.

Often the installation of specialised manufacturing equipment favoured a particular technique for future designs. Round tube provided lightness and strength in many implements until steel-makers started producing rectangular hollow

Above: The introduction of the tractor posed other problems for implement manufacturers. Even the little Ivel was more powerful than a team of horses, but the irresistible nature of the pull meant that shock loads were imposed on the implement frame. No binder was designed to tow a second binder, as here, so additional unexpected loads would be placed on the front machine. Within a few years designs would have to take account of these extra stresses.

Right: Marshall's of Gainsborough was an early pioneer of internal combustion tractors. Its Colonial model was too powerful for the British market in 1908, but sold in areas where use of steam was hampered by shortages of fuel or water. A branch office was even set up in Saskatchewan, Canada, to back sales to the Canadian Prairies.

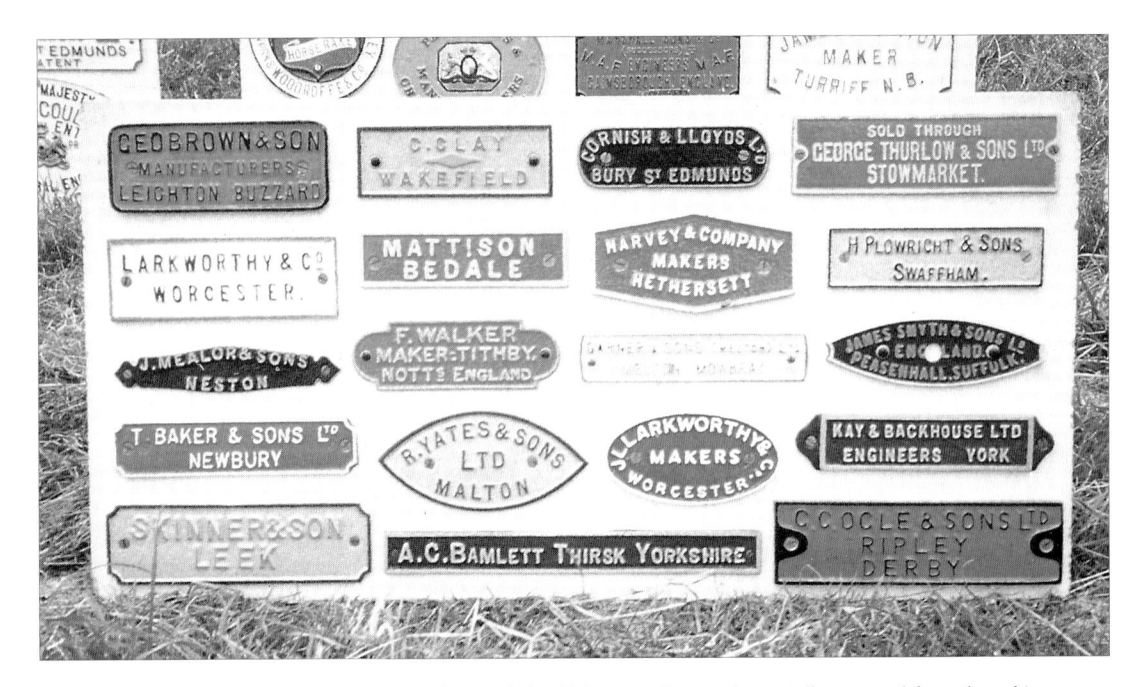

Above: The cast-iron maker's plate was a rugged way of identifying a product, and especially on wood-framed machinery was often the longest-lasting part. Collectors are restoring and displaying these to make a thought-provoking roll-call of bygone makers, some of whom still survive as dealers rather than manufacturers.

Below: Sometimes a firm customer's order preceded implement development work. A keen salesman took an order for a Fendt tool carrier, but to clinch the order a seven-unit gang-mower had to be fitted. The finished job proved quick and easy to use and was a good example of co-operation between the supplier, his fabrication department and the customer. While some parts were bought in, others were taken from existing machinery belonging to the customer. Further orders followed.

Above: Factory-fitted safety cabs as on this Massey Ferguson 590 meant that implement designers had to consider the clearance space needed for the cab itself, as well as the fact that farmers often wanted to use existing implements with a new tractor. Most problems arose from fouling opening doors and windows; driver's misjudgements tended to result in broken glass.

sections (RHS). These 'square tubes' proved quicker and easier to fabricate, so makers changed their designs to utilise them. Yet no individual implement manufacturer could have justified the investment needed to introduce RHS.

Likely sales can also influence the decision of whether to manufacture or to buy in. Suppose an agricultural engineer meets several potential customers with a similar requirement. The conventional advice would be to offer a suitable implement from an established supplier. But what if that is not what the customer really requires? Suppose he is willing to pay? It might be worth the engineer buying in some components to build exactly the machine the customer wants. We will see examples of this approach in crop-sprayers and mechanical handling, and it is how so many different firms got into making self-propelled crop-sprayers and forklift trucks.

Sometimes the law restricts manufacture. Today tractors are required to be fitted with a safety cab, which has to be tested to confirm that it meets legal requirements to protect an operator. Few companies would have the finance to get a cab made and approved for a small production run, so no small companies are involved in tractor manufacture. In the same way engines and axles now have to be Type Approved, and as a result are bought in from specialist suppliers.

When a new implement is introduced, at first predicted sales are small. The design process for the first prototype may be little more than a sketch or some chalk lines drawn on the workshop floor, which can work well if the designer is also the chap that is doing the fabrication. This prototype may well work but it is likely to be heavy and crude looking. Often the first customers and users join in the design process.

Once designers get involved much more attention is given to designing out weight and cost. This will show itself in each component being more closely

Below: Instead of fitting an implement to a tractor, a few makers tried fitting a tractor to an implement. In this case a self-propelled potato harvester is driven and powered by a Ford tractor. From the designer's point of view the engine, transmission and other components could be bought in as one unit. Once the designer became more confident later designs would usually feature even more sophisticated power and transmission components. Often this followed pressure from early customers for the maker to be more adventurous in design terms.

17

Above: **Sometimes designers fail to anticipate the eventual use of their product. Bearing in mind that a Ferguson tractor weighed just over a ton and had a top speed of around 12mph, never in their wildest dreams would the designers have anticipated their trailer being used behind a tractor of 150hp and capable of over 40mph! Of course much the same jump happened when traditional wooden horse-wagons were hitched to Fergusons 50 years ago.**

Below: **Sometimes an agricultural tractor provides a starting point for industrial machinery. This hefty crane is built around an International B450 tractor, but with a lifting capacity of up to 5 tons it can move only on a smooth, hard surface. Crude it may be, but it has provided a cost-effective answer to the demand for a cheap yard crane.**

matched to the predicted stresses. Unfortunately, if the designer does not have an extensive agricultural background he may discover later that users mistreat equipment and subject it to more than the predicted stresses!

Sometimes identifying a limited need is the clue to much more potential. Once Joe Bamford started making loaders, good design and salesmanship made his company grow. Although aiming initially at farmers, he soon specialised in the construction market, but then became aware that many farmers were buying second-hand machines for use on the farm, which eventually was to bring him back into

Left: Importing offers a way for a small firm to offer sophisticated machinery. Two ingredients are vital for success: a quality machine that meets a genuine need, and an effective long-term working relationship between a supportive factory and an enthusiastic agent who genuinely believes in the product. Here, at the end of a hot day at the Royal Show in 1977, the late Fred Tuck strikes a pose for the camera while lowering the Fendt flag on Bill Bennett Engineering Ltd's stand.

Below: Rather than starting to manufacture reversible ploughs, Bamford imported the Kevernland range; the Zetor Crystal tractor was also imported, in this case from Czechoslovakia. Farmers and dealers were beginning to consider imported alternatives to British-built equipment. *RLM*

the agricultural market. While H. Cameron Gardner made nearly as substantial a loader as JCB, it tended to focus only on the needs of agricultural users.

For some customers the answer might be to modify an existing machine. Suppose a farmer felt that his existing tractor and loader were too small for his needs. One answer would be to buy in a used construction machine that could be modified for agricultural use. For example, several firms specialised in supplying dung forks to fit mass-produced hydraulic digger/loaders.

Maybe a customer might need something even more specialised, for apple-growing, perhaps, or

Above: The Kevernland design relied on a central heat-treated rectangular beam with individual legs attached, which made a stronger frame for a big plough. The stresses and strains generated when ploughing at speed would be too much for traditional bolted construction.

Below: Legrand was a French maker of muck-spreaders seeking a good agent in 1975. With Britain joining the Common Market, continental makers foresaw opportunities to sell their machinery in Britain. The tractor was also imported, the 1080 being borrowed from the Massey Ferguson demonstration fleet.

hops, or brussels sprouts. With such a limited potential the choice would be between building implements in very small numbers or contacting a manufacturer in another country who might offer a suitable machine that could be imported. In this way an agricultural engineer in a small way of business could become a specialist, whether as an importer or a manufacturer.

Importing could also be the answer in the early stages of demand. As we will see in Chapter 4, imported ploughs tended to be available in larger sizes than British-made examples, and were too big to suit most mass-produced British tractors. Since British plough-makers concentrated on that market, they left an opening for the importing of larger ploughs to suit the bigger tractors made in small numbers by County, Muir-Hill and Roadless, for example.

If a small manufacturer was faced with a sudden redesign of its products, importing might again be useful; after all, the sales staff knew many of the potential customers and also had contact with local dealers. While a sugar-beet harvester was still painted a familiar colour, it may have come from a different factory. In the author's *An Illustrated History of Combine Harvesters* (Ian Allan Publishing, 2001) we saw how, while the name stayed the same, the factory that made the combine might change for commercial reasons.

Conversely, some companies were set up with the backing of an overseas maker to provide it with an outlet in Britain. In other cases the maker might buy out its original importer to establish what was effectively a branch office, if in its judgement the

Above: Larger implements required larger tractors. The Marshall name was revived for what had been the Leyland range of tractors. To add interest to their stand at Smithfield one year they featured an early Colonial tractor that had been repatriated. When you look at its size you see why in its day it was considered too big for British farms.

Below: With a powerful tractor like this County on the front, even a big plough could be pulled fast enough to produce well-broken furrows. To meet this requirement Ransomes introduced its four-furrow reversible TS89 in 1969, for which it reverted to bolted construction. One advantage was that a dismantled plough made a compact consignment for export shipping. *RLM*

Above: The arrival of bigger imported tractors like this TW25 meant that makers could build bigger implements for higher output. Early attempts to mount implements on the front of a tractor usually involved the manufacturer designing and fabricating mounting brackets to suit each individual model. In this case a front-mounted topper takes the leaves off beet before they are lifted by the trailed machine. The specified twin narrow wheels straddle one row of growing beet without damaging it.

potential sales in Britain would be sufficient to keep implement costs down by making and selling them in larger numbers.

Probably the biggest single pressure on a maker is, of course, whether farmers will buy its products. Reasons for not buying include poor profits in the previous year - the existing equipment does nearly as good a job - and capital being needed for some other essential improvement on the farm. The most potent factor is that another maker is offering a better way of doing the same job; there is little point in introducing a new tractor loader if most customers are buying specialised handlers instead. Often the best designed and most effective implement is introduced just as demand is moving on to a different way of doing the same job.

It is when the buying decision is being made that a dealer's representative can have a crucial effect. He can either supply the customer with what he asks for, or suggest a better and more economic way of doing the job. A good 'rep' has a well-established reputation with local farmers, for in the long run scrupulous honesty has always been the best policy. Of course, the makes and types of machinery for which his employer holds an agency may influence him, but even more important, he will be urged if possible to move unsold machinery held in stock.

One curious help with implement sales is what might be called the 'ratchet effect'. A farmer buys a tractor and an implement to work with it. Under difficult conditions the tractor struggles to operate the implement. To overcome this the farmer replaces his tractor with a more powerful model. While it now operates the implement, the increased power being applied is causing extra wear on the implement. The answer is a new, stronger and bigger implement. Now once again the tractor is left struggling with the implement under difficult conditions. The only answer is a larger tractor, and so the process goes on. Every change of implement or tractor is aimed at speeding up the job in some way, and it is this constant desire for better and faster ways of doing jobs that drives implement sales.

Since most implements are used only for a short season each year, a manufacturer has to ensure that supplies are available before the critical season or

Right: Sometimes an implement design solution arrives after the problem has gone away. Mangolds and fodder beet used to provide winter feed especially for the period after Christmas. Lifting, carting and storing them was hard work often under unpleasant muddy conditions. As a result, most farms began to rely on silage, and the area of those two crops has fallen. However, by making use of a modern sugar-beet harvester the job could be mechanised. Their high cost meant that few were used on other crops until they were becoming less popular.

Below right: In work the roots are lifted up and out of the ground by two belts gripping the leaves. As they pass through the machine the roots are cut free and conveyed into a bunker, while the leaves are discharged to the rear.
By altering the chute, the leaves can be left in rows.

Bottom: This design was developed by the Irish Sugar Company for harvesting sugar beet grown on small farms. As the tops are cut after the root is out of the ground, the machine can also be used on vegetable crops such as beetroot, carrots and parsnips. With more potential users, the sales prospects are slightly better. The bunker can be emptied hydraulically into a trailer for carting back to the farm.

Above: Certain soils in South Africa respond to very deep ripping to break up pans. On a big farm, this needs a powerful tractor and a very substantial implement. Visiting salesmen from overseas sometimes feel that their customers are exaggerating their requirements, hence this locally fabricated ripper cultivator and a 614kW (800hp) ACO 600 tractor on the front. Sometimes local suppliers have the best idea of local needs. RLM

the order could be missed. This seasonal use means that there is only a limited opportunity to try out prototypes each year. As well as these specific factors, an implement-maker has to face the same commercial problems as any other manufacturing business.

If the implements meet farmers' needs, and farmers are in a position to buy, the implement company is likely to flourish. However, when farming is going through hard times or the makers' products are outclassed or undercut by competitors, it is likely to go into a decline. We will see examples of this when we look at trailers.

Below: Not every brilliant implement idea gets the sales it deserves. The Dowler gantry was a novel approach to reducing soil compaction. Shown here parked in the travel position, the wheels could rotate through 90° so that in work the wheel track was 36ft (11m) wide. When the implement had covered the full width of the field the whole gantry was moved sideways by its working width, with one set of wheels now running in the track previously used by the other. Between the wheels nothing had run over the soil, so its structure was unaffected. Advisors, researchers and writers all hailed this as a great step forward, but unfortunately, while there was great interest, insufficient orders were placed by farmers willing to invest in the system, so little more has been heard of the gantry.

Right: Hedges form a natural renewable field boundary. In time they become straggly. To make them stockproof once again they require specialist attention.

Centre right: Not every job can yet be done by the use of an implement. To keep a hedge trim and stockproof it should be laid, which needs to be done only every 30-50 years. Despite all the ingenious machines, this is still a farm job best done by hand, although admittedly a chain-saw makes the first part of the job easier. Hedge-laying used to be accepted as a skill that most farm workers possessed, but today it is mainly done by enthusiasts with a pride in their countryside. It is very easy to say 'something should be done about hedges', but only a few people will go out and get scratched and cold on a winter's day to do what is needed.

Below right: The uprights that remain are partly severed, bent over and staked into position. Despite appearances, this is not vandalism. This stretch was last done about 30 years ago. The uprights bent over then have produced numerous uprights, which thicken the hedge. As Leicestershire is hunting country the local hunts used to encourage hedge-laying with the aim of improving the jumps into fields; few farmers could otherwise justify the costs when margins were tight. The large field enclosed by this hedge was once a complete farm subdivided into several fields; the internal hedges were removed long ago, and it is now just a single field within a much bigger farm.

3. Before tractors: Horse and Steam

Above: A young horseman takes a closer look at the shafts of a typical cart. The shafts are bent and shaped to accommodate a carthorse; a well-made set will hardly touch the horse, but will provide suitable attachment points for the horse's harness.

At the start of the 20th century horses still reigned supreme as motive power. When you consider the advantages they offered it is easy to see why. For fuel they ran on home-grown grass in the summer and hay in the winter, while oats grown on the farm provided the extra energy needed when working hard.

In the easygoing accounting systems adopted by farmers, that meant that the fuel cost was nil. Once a farmer was established it was rare for him to need to buy replacement horses, as a suitable mare could be got in foal. One of the horsemen would welcome the challenge of breaking the youngster to harness at two or three years old, and soon the farm would have another replacement power unit. Accordingly most implements were designed to be operated by one or more horses, and horse-drawn implements therefore make a good starting point for us.

Certainly horses did have their disadvantages. For example, they needed looking after, but good horsemen could be engaged very cheaply and few farmers worried about the cost of labour. Repairs and replacements were needed, but every village had a nearby blacksmith who could fit shoes as required. By today's standards horses were slow, but few countrymen travelled at more than walking pace.

The threat to horse-drawn implements was expected to come from steam, and in particular the

Above: Like a tractor, a horse has a form of 'three-point hitch'. The actual pull is exerted from the collar, which should be carefully matched and padded to the horse's physique so that the load is well distributed over the horse's shoulders. Since it would be difficult to attach a towing point firmly to the collar itself, the pull is transmitted by chain via the hames, the two curved metal bars round the collar. The shafts of the cart or implement need to be supported or these front chains would tend to dangle down and interfere with the horse's legs, therefore a chain passing over the saddle is employed to support the shafts. A third chain from the shafts is attached to the breech strap, the broad strap around the horse's rump. This chain has two jobs: when the horse backs up it helps to reverse the implement, and when descending a hill it transmits the horse's braking power to the cart or implement. Note that with the horse at rest, the front chain is hanging slack while the rear chain is under tension.

ploughing engine. Here was equipment that could do as much work as 20 teams of two or three horses each day. While this was impressive, a farmer would still need to find winter work for the men and horses even if the ploughing was done by other means; few farmers could afford to buy the equipment for cable ploughing, and much of the work was done by contractors, who felt that they never gained as much work as they had hoped. Steam engines were enjoying greater success driving and transporting threshing machines, an aspect covered in detail in *An Illustrated History of Combine Harvesters*.

Dan Albone's Ivel 'Agricultural Motor' was the first British tractor running on petrol. Sales were slow and at first it had little impact on most farms. At the 1902 Royal Show it came under the eye of a forward-looking judge, Mr Dugdale. What was so striking about his report was the calm way in which it was accepted that the tractor would be the way forward. Here was a machine of totally novel design, yet it was accepted as an effective way of doing the job. Bearing in mind that he had no previous experience with agricultural tractors, Dugdale's reservations were most perceptive. He was concerned about the effect of the weight of the back wheels on the soil, but he did suggest that the wheels would not puddle the soil as badly as a team of heavy horses. To avoid running wheels over ploughed ground he felt that a horse team would still be needed to finish off each 'land' of ploughing. Another concern was the risk of allowing farm employees to work with petrol; farmers were advised to check their insurance position first.

Left: Brakes were usually crude on farm wagons. The skid on a chain or 'the drag' under the wheel will be run over as the wagon moves forward, and with its chain tight the wheel effectively becomes a skid. While this was effective when the wagon was moving forward, it did not prevent it from rolling back. A looped chain around the wheel prevented much movement of the wheel in either direction, but of course could only be applied when the wagon was stationary. Years later some trailers were offered with hand-brakes that were also only to be applied when the outfit was stationary.

For greater strength wagon wheels were made with a slight dish, and the axle was inclined slightly so that the spoke nearest the ground was vertical. Since this spoke was in compression carrying the load, this was the strongest arrangement. A bonus was that since the tops of the wheels were further apart, either a wider body could be fitted or there was more clearance between the wheels and the body. This example is part of the Cotswold Countryside Collection at Northleach, Gloucestershire.

Below left: Typically a wagon's front wheels were made smaller than the rear so that they could pass under the body to permit the wagon to make a tighter turn. The drag is carried ready for use hanging by its chain in front of the rear wheels. These drags tended to damage roads and their use was prohibited by many local bylaws. This was a waste of time, as few carters would consider a bylaw more important than the well-being of their teams! This wagon was seen at the Three Counties Show in 2000.

Right: For some jobs one horse would not have sufficient pull. Here the main pull to the implement comes from the trace chains. The harness is a relatively modern American type, used by working horse enthusiasts. The implement is a riding cultivator; many similar implements would have been modified for use behind early tractors.

Left: Wagon tyres took the wear and tear from travel over a metalled road, and were normally thick enough to last for the life of the wheel. At the blacksmith's the correct length of flat strip was bent into a circle with the aid of the hand-cranked bending rollers seen on the left. When the two ends were fire-welded in the forge it formed a ring that was slightly smaller in diameter than the wheel it was to fit. When the wooden components of the wheel had been assembled, the ring would be heated, and thus its diameter would increase. When the blacksmith judged that it was hot enough, the tyre would be lowered over the wheel and hammered into place. Cold water would then be poured on to prevent the wood burning. This also cooled the tyre, and as it shrank back to its original diameter it exerted a vice-like grip on the wheel. A similar technique is still used to fit starter ring gears to the flywheel of an engine. The equipment shown is exhibited at the Cotswold Countryside Collection.

Above: Another way of applying a second horse was to put a trace horse in front; this was a quick way of providing assistance over heavy going, but only the rear horse could provide any braking on a descent. This arrangement was popular where one horse could cope with the load most of the time but needed some assistance, for example up a steep hill. It was relatively easy to clip the extra trace horse on to give that extra assistance and detach it again when the problem had been overcome. Another advantage was that the horses both walked in the same track, which also matched the track of a horse pulling a two-wheeled cart.

The power of the horse is applied through the substantial collar, which fits over and slides down the neck and takes up a position against the breastbone. When correctly made, the collar is an accurate fit to the profile of a particular horse and is appropriately padded so that it rests comfortably without risk of causing sores. The trace chains then pass back through a simple strap over the horse's back and over the rear haunches to prevent them fouling the horse's legs. Steering of the front horse is effected either by the rope reins, which are taken right back to the wagon, or by a second horseman walking alongside.

Below left: For an implement with a seat, rope reins would often be appropriate. With the horse stopped, the ropes are relaxed allowing the horse to look round and enjoy the parade in which it is taking part at Ripley Show in North Yorkshire. The implement is a two-row swathe turner for drying hay.

Above and right: Leading a horse like this was usual in the field and made a good first job for youngsters. One hazard was that any lapse in concentration might mean the horse treading heavily and painfully on the leader's foot! At first sight the horse is pulling a typical farm wagon, but it is in fact a two-wheeled cart modified to take a bulky load of hay or sheaves. The front axle is pivoted, yet it and its superstructure can quickly be removed to leave a two-wheeled cart for carrying dung, roots and other heavier loads. No extra weight was imposed on the horse. Known as 'hermaphrodites', these carts were never common, but were an early example of a multi-purpose trailer. The steering lock was limited; too tight a turn meant the front wheel striking the centre bar, a problem that still occurs on modern trailers.

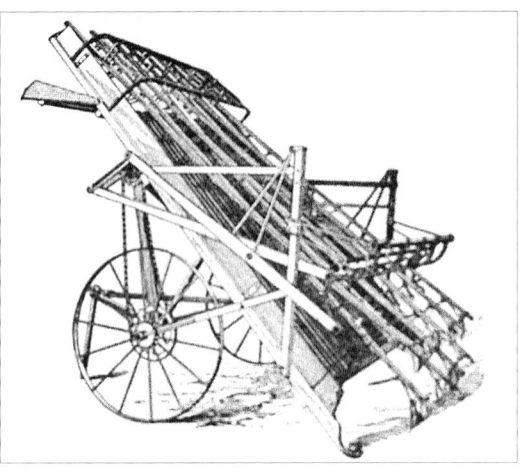

This page: This cart has also been modified to increase its carrying capacity, with extensions fitted to the front and sides. The implement behind and seen in the drawing is a hay-loader; as it is towed forward behind the cart it rakes and lifts hay up into body for the stacker to deal with. The hay-loader lifted the big load in the photograph in 9 minutes, which would have represented sustained hard work for the two-horse team. Although it looks to be imposing an excessive load on the rear horse, it is slightly counterbalanced by the extra depth of the load at the back.

For the first time it was possible to achieve mechanical power on the farm without the use of a steam engine. This was very much a leap into the unknown for most farmers, although they would have been aware of the very first motor cars that just occasionally were to be seen on the road. Indeed, they may have heard reports of an American traction engine powered by a petrol engine.

Dan Albone's vision was that his 'Agricultural Motor' could be used to take on the work previously carried out by horses. He even talked wildly that it could replace horse teams. To most farmers, who took a great pride in their horses, this seemed like heresy.

With hindsight we can see that Dan Albone's vision was to be proved correct. His argument was that a motor did not tire like a horse. It would continue to do the same amount of work hour after hour, or indeed until the driver got tired. What he may not have realised was how long it would be before his wild ideas were fully accepted.

Meanwhile the wagon and team remained an important means of transport to the nearest town or railway station. The four-wheeled wagon was the preferred transport for bigger loads and longer journeys. There were pronounced regional variations in the design of wagons, stemming from the demands of local farmers and the fact that a wheelwright or wagon-builder may have served his apprenticeship locally, so that was the design with which he was most familiar.

Steering was normally effected by the front end of the wagon bodywork having a substantial frame and a circular rubbing plate that dropped on to and matched a similar plate on a wooden platform built up above the front axle; the horses' movement in the shafts effected a direct turning action on this turntable. Although this layout may appear crude, it had a number of merits. While they had a long life expectancy, such wagons could be built locally using local timber. A wagon was easy to repair in the event of damage, and greasing the wheels and turntable reduced the load on the horse(s) considerably. Strength with lightness was important to customers, and a spokeshave would be used to remove all excess weight from the timbers used to build up the turntable and the wagon frame.

Above: With so many collectors of old machinery, some amazing implements have survived into preservation. This is a Houseman horse-drawn hedge-slasher of 1900. As the horse ambles along the giant blade spins at high speed behind, slashing through overgrown hedges. Inevitably the horse would be struck by the odd hedge trimming, and while it did apparently work, it must have needed a mighty placid horse! Looking at the drive system, there is no provision for a free wheel, so the momentum of the spinning blade would tend to propel the machine forward, which again must have been disconcerting for the horse trying to stop!

Left: Rutherfords made this mower in the early 1900s. When photographed it had just been brought from Poland for sale at an Old Sodbury's Sortout, where all sorts of old and unlikely farm junk is bought and sold. The improvised repair to the wheel attracted admiring comment.

Above: Bamfords of Uttoxeter was rather better known for their mowers, and while clearly originally horse-drawn, this mower has been converted to tractor operation with a modification to the drawbar. In the shed at the back of the display at Cogges Farm Museum is an early Samuelson sail reaper.

Below: This horse-drawn implement has been blacksmith-modified to fit the three-point linkage on this David Brown Cropmaster. It is a root drill using conical rollers to ride on two ridges while also driving a vertical shaft through a bevel gear. At the top of the shaft another, hidden, bevel gear meshes with the crown wheel that has a choice of three tracks. This shaft drives the two seed units, which feed seed down the tubes to the slot in the ground made by the shaped iron deflectors. Sowing seeds on the ridge like this made it easier to hoe weeds. This represented a light job even for a single horse walking up the furrow between the two ridges; with a tractor attached as shown, the wheels would have run on the ridges, but in use they could be repositioned to alter their spacing to fit in adjoining furrows. In view of the time and trouble needed, root drilling would have remained a horse job as long as a useful horse and horseman persisted on the farm. This example was seen at the Blue Cross Rally held in Oxfordshire in 2000.

Above: Carts built with pneumatic tyres were lighter to pull or could carry a greater load for the same number of horses. At the same time bodybuilding was becoming much simpler with the use of purchased steel brackets as corner pieces and axle supports.

Research in the 1930s found that pneumatic tyres on horse-drawn equipment reduced the rolling resistance. This either made the horse's job easier or allowed more weight to be hauled for the same effort.

A carter always had mixed emotions about a trip into town. Here was his chance to turn his charges out in finest style to show his pride in his horses and his master, but this pride was tempered by the knowledge that his display could catch the eye of a horse-dealer. A well-trained and broken farmhorse met a ready demand for town work by hauliers looking for replacements for their stables. No horseman liked losing a horse he had trained, but a good sale represented a useful income for the farm; most had a good youngster coming on, and breeding their own replacements on the farm is one trick tractor-users have still not mastered!

Today we tend to think that a horse could not generate enough useful power for farm work. Yet before the arrival of tractors they provided enough power for farms, and it would be another 40 years before horsepower began to be regarded as old-fashioned on a commercial farm.

Right: The first use of steam was in the form of the portable engine, which could be towed from farm to farm by one or two horses. Once in position and steam raised, most portables could generate more power at the flywheel than several horses. While this was a step forward, its use was limited to driving threshing machines and chaff-cutters. Few farms could justify the cost of a steam engine for everyday use.

Above and below: Even when tractors were becoming more popular the steam engine builders did not give up easily. Garrett of Leiston, in Suffolk, offered a steam engine intended for direct traction work pulling an implement. The Suffolk Punch, with its unconventional layout, was designed as a steam agricultural tractor, but sadly it proved nothing like as popular as the breed of horse after which it was named. While the driving position did give better forward visibility, the driver would have little idea of what was happening behind.

4. Ploughing: The Start of the Farming Year

Any operation that involves contact with and moving the soil is generally referred to as cultivation. Without some form of cultivation little of value would grow and be fit for harvesting; it is no exaggeration to say that without cultivation the world would starve within a year.

The most distinctive form of cultivation is ploughing. A field's appearance is transformed under a plough. The topsoil, which is where plants grow, and where the main fertility is stored, is lifted and turned over in some way.

Ploughing is the starting point for preparing the soil to get it into the best condition to receive seed for the next crop. First the ploughshare passes through and separates the top layer of soil, then a disc or knife coulter cuts this soil free from the main mass. Finally the action of the mouldboard lifts the soil up and over so that it is less compacted and air can get in. Turning over the soil buries any weeds that were on the surface, which makes it more difficult for them to continue growing, thus reducing competition suffered by the next crop. Any plant residues or other organic matter buried will break down, usually adding fertility. The loosening also helps surplus water to percolate down into the soil where it can be absorbed; moisture that drains away is of no use for future growth, and it may even wash nutrients out of the soil. The uneven surface left by the furrow also means that a far greater area of soil is exposed to weathering.

Right: This group of illustrations from an old textbook in the author's collection shows early developments in plough design. The first (1.) shows a basic ground scratcher plough, which disturbs rather than inverts the soil. The second (2.) is a typical plough of the late 17th century; most of the frame would be of suitable bent timbers. By the middle of the 18th century wheels were being added (3.), but to our eyes the design is still very crude. Adding a second trace horse (4.) increases the power available, allowing the plough to work to a greater depth. The more advanced design of plough used in the Home Counties around the middle of the 18th century (5.) has twin front wheels and a straight frame, suggesting that the effort needed to pull it has been reduced.

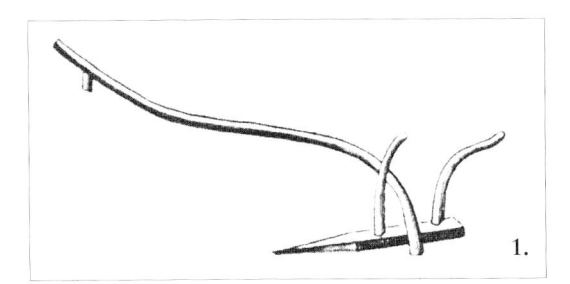

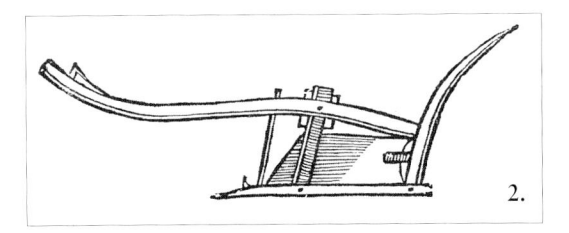

Below and inset left: Many rural pubs use old implements as a combined decoration and sign. At the Black Horse near Calne in Wiltshire a horse-drawn ridger has been mounted over the entrance porch. The handles carry the identification plate of the dealer, T. H. White's, which is still an important agricultural engineering firm throughout Wiltshire. The spanner clips are original but the left-hand spanner is rather more modern than the original spanner provided. Spanners supplied with machines formed the starting point of the first limited collection of tools on many farms.

Left: Ruston and Hornsby of Lincoln built this two-furrow plough which would have needed at least three horses to pull it. It retained the handles so that the ploughman continued to walk behind.

Ploughing on its own is rarely enough to produce ideal growing conditions for the next crop. Sometimes you will notice a field that has been ploughed then left neglected, as it appears, for months at a time. The farmer is taking advantage of the weather to assist with the breaking up of the soil ready to produce good growing conditions for the next crop. Frost is a great ally of the farmer. Water that has accumulated in the soil freezes, and the ice expands, tending to split the soil apart; burst pipes demonstrate the extremely powerful splitting action of freezing water! Freezing also plays a major part in the formation of soil as rocks are broken down, but this is such a long, slow process that we may not be aware that it is still happening.

The significance of frost depends on the type of soil. When wet, sticky clay has been ploughed in the winter it looks unpromising, but heavy frosts mean that next spring those solid furrows will be relatively light and crumbly, and will break down surprisingly rapidly when the correct implements are used to produce the tilth.

Ploughs have evolved from suitably shaped tree branches being dragged through the soil. At first they did little more than form a groove in the soil, but development led to the classic type of plough where the soil is cut, lifted and inverted.

In Britain development of the iron plough is generally credited to Ransomes of Ipswich, and particularly to that firm's invention of the chilled

Above: A typically neat job from Douglas Reed with a Ransomes match plough. Extra fittings are the two rollers that firm the furrows into place, while the long mouldboards are producing furrows that are almost unbroken, and all the stubble on the surface is being buried.

Below: The two cranks on the plough turn threaded rods to adjust the plough, altering the quality of the work. This type of ploughing is known as 'high cut' or 'longboard', and is no longer needed commercially. If seed was scattered on the furrows after a winter of weathering a single pass with the harrows would be sufficient to cover the seed for near ideal growing conditions. Seeing such work in competitions spurred commercial ploughmen to make a

iron share. An American, of course, would give the credit to John Deere and his iron plough. There have been many variations of plough body over the years, but always the aim has been to produce the type of furrow that the farmer requires while minimising the draught or load on the animal or tractor pulling the plough. Also, the speed at which the plough travels affects the shape of the furrow it leaves. For a tractor plough designer there are a considerable number of possibilities.

The amount of effort needed to pull even a single-furrow plough through the soil at a reasonable working depth often meant that more than one horse was needed to pull it. At first most ploughs were manufactured to cut single furrows, and the number of horses would vary according to the type of soil.

In the United States there was a need for one man to be able to operate more than one horse; with plenty of horses but a shortage of manpower, this was the only way of getting more work done in a day. This led to the introduction of the two-furrow plough, and with it came an innovation that shocked most British farmers - the suggestion that the operator should ride on the plough rather than walk behind it.

Walking behind a horse-plough is far more demanding than it might appear. First of all the ploughman has to control the horse(s) by means of reins linked to the horse's head. Where teams are being used this might also involve linking the horses' heads together by a rein or strap so that they will turn and operate in unison. In addition, the operator has the plough handles to control, and these can buck considerably when stones or other obstacles are hit. Appreciable effort is needed from the ploughman to correct the action of the plough, direct it, and achieve the correct working depth.

At the same time the ploughman has to walk across the field following the plough. This is relatively straightforward on dry, light soil, but on a sticky, wet clay field in the middle of November large amounts of soil will build up on his boots, and he will soon be walking along with extra weight attached around his ankles. He is also walking within a furrow, so there is only restricted space in which to place his feet; each foot must be placed in front of the other, and at each step has to be lifted right out of the furrow, around and down. No wonder that by the end of the day the ploughman used to plod his weary way home!

Moreover, he has far more than his ploughing to think about, for he is also in charge of the horse team. This means that before work starts in the morning the team may have to be got in from the field or fed in the stable, groomed, checked over for any ailments, given water, and harnessed ready to set off to the field. This will have called for an early start, before dawn perhaps, by the light of a single lantern. Once the team is prepared they will have to be led or walked to the field where the plough is waiting, and hooked on.

At the end of the day, after ploughing is completed, the team will have to be taken back to their stable, given another feed, watered, then either turned out to the field or bedded up in the stable for the night. And this isn't the end of the job. At least one of the horsemen will need to visit the horses later that night to make sure that all is well with them.

Depending on local custom there would be one or two breaks in the day. The team would pause briefly to receive their feed in nosebags, while the ploughman would make himself comfortable under a suitable tree or hedge and snatch a quick bite

Below: To encourage competitive ploughing Ransomes offered these ornate 'Certificates of Merit' for winners who had used Ransomes' ploughs.

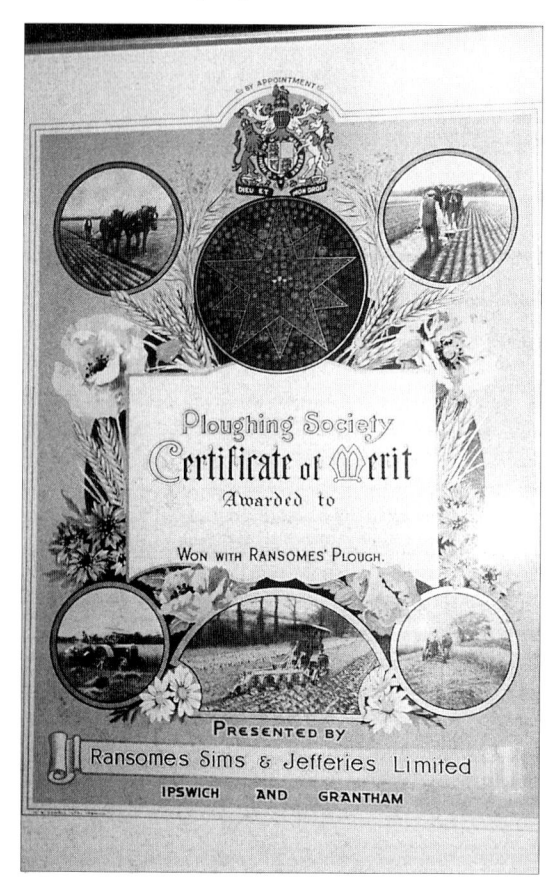

Above and below: The steam plough was the first successful attempt to mechanise the job. The steersman controls the plough as it travels almost silently across the field. The plough is built double-ended so that it can plough in both directions. (The passenger is hitching a precarious lift in traditional style.) Power for the plough comes from a pair of steam ploughing engines; massive winches under the boilers wind or unwind the cable, drawing the plough backwards and forwards across the field. At the end of each pull the plough is lifted out of work and the leading end is pulled down to the ground. Once the steersman is aboard, the other engine drags the plough back across the field.

washed down with beer or cold tea. In some parts of the country such a break is still known as 'baggin (nosebagging) time' or 'llowance (allowance) time'.

Typically this break would only be half an hour, then it would be back to the unrelenting grind until knocking-off time. This was the prospect that faced the ploughman day after long weary day in the autumn and winter, preparing fields for next year's crop.

Why would anybody accept such a terrible-sounding job? The cynical answer is that they knew no better. Indeed, many ploughmen grew up to the job following in their father's footsteps. There were, however, compensations. You were out in the open air. You were working with horses, who could offer a considerable amount of companionship to a ploughman who appreciated their company. There was also a fierce pride in the job of work being done. They knew that their neighbours and fellow workers would be studying the quality of their work, and they would be offered advice, criticism and good-humoured jokes if any shortcomings were observed.

This pride in a good job still shows itself in ploughing matches, which often originated from the custom of being a good neighbour. When a new farmer moved into a farm he would face a backlog of ploughing, as the outgoing farmer would probably have been behind with his work. The new farmer would need some time to get established and get his men and horses organised. The practice therefore grew up that neighbours would offer the farmer a day's ploughing with their teams to help

Above: In drier climates steam engines were used to pull ploughs direct. By pulling four separate ploughs, 16 furrows are here being turned in one pass. These are clearly shallow furrows in soil that has already been cultivated.

Left and below: The working area at the annual Great Dorset Steam Fair at Tarrant Hinton is intensively cultivated, but offers the chance to see some unusual machines at work. As late as 1915 tractor design was still evolving. This early design of Case with a single driven rear wheel is being demonstrated with a two-furrow plough. Not surprisingly, most farmers still favoured real horsepower.

Above right: Based in Bedfordshire, Howard was well placed to make ploughs for early tractors. This two-furrow version dates from around World War 1 and is seen here in action 80 years later. The two outer levers adjust the depth wheels, while the middle lever is to steer the front wheel. The International Junior tractor dates from rather later, the early 1920s.

him on with the field work in that first year. By custom, all the teams would visit the farm on the same day, and perhaps ten, a dozen or even 20 teams would be in the same field tackling the same conditions. Inevitably, good-humoured rivalry grew up between the ploughmen - all were anxious to show off their best possible work. From these informal beginnings ploughing societies started, organising matches where the ploughmen all met up on a given day to compete against each other for cups and trophies awarded by farmers and landowners. There was another very practical side to such competitions: local farmers would notice a good ploughman, and this would stand him in good stead if he needed to change employer. Competition ploughing still continues as a rural activity, and often there will be classes for both modern equipment and older outfits.

There had been a mechanical alternative to horse-ploughing since the 1880s. John Fowler pioneered steam ploughing. Self-propelled steam engines fitted with large winding drums were used to haul a massive plough back and forth across a field, turning between four and seven furrows at a time. The high cost of the equipment made this a contract service that was most cost-effective for large areas with big fields.

Steam ploughing was usually deeper than regular ploughing, and might only be undertaken one year in four. Once the equipment was on site it was quick, and since the steamers stayed on the edge of the field there was little risk of damage to the soil structure. By the start of the 20th century steam ploughing contractors were operating in most important arable areas. Demand was at its highest during World War 1, but declined during the 1920s and 1930s, with a revival for land reclamation during World War 2.

While steam ploughing was normally a contract operation, many farmers could afford a tractor once they had convinced themselves they needed one. When tractors came on the scene, ploughing was seen as a natural task for them.

At first the ploughs used were little different from horse-ploughs, simply towed with a chain. The American riding plough, previously mentioned, offered more output. If the tractor could cope, one could be trailed behind, still probably attached by a chain, but requiring a second man to ride on it. His jobs included operating the lifting and lowering controls at the start and finish of work, keeping an

Below: Spuds are fitted to the plough wheel to ensure drive to the hub mechanism on the right. The first tug on the spring-controlled lever allows the plough to drop down. The next tug lets the rotating wheel drive the lift mechanism as the plough moves forward.

eye on the operation of the plough and steering it to ensure that it followed a clean furrow.

After a few years it was found practical to attach the plough by means of a rigid drawbar, bringing it closer to the towing tractor. Now the tractor could turn in a tighter circle, and less ground had to be left at the end of the ploughing for the 'headland' (the turning area). The operation of the controls was also altered so that the tractor driver himself could control the plough, helped by the introduction of the mechanical trip. When a rope or lever was pulled, the rotation of one of the plough wheels, working through a mechanism, lifted the plough out of work and secured it with a latch. The next tug on the same rope or lever released the latch and permitted the plough to drop back into work at the start of the next furrow.

Tractor ploughing was a great relief for horses, but was certainly not universally welcomed. For one thing, a tractor was heavier than a horse and it was felt that the wheels would leave ruts in the field and spoil the condition of the soil. Early tractors struggled for grip under wet and slippery conditions, and often had to stop work altogether when horses could have continued to plough effectively.

Suppose the ploughing was now completed more quickly. What work were the horsemen to do during the winter? Few farms were willing to rely solely on tractor ploughing, so there were still horse-ploughmen to be kept employed. A typical early compromise was to use the tractor for the

Above: A closer look at a trailed plough. The long shiny part is the mouldboard; the polish comes from the friction of the soil as the mouldboard passes beneath it while lifting and turning the furrow. As this is a special model for use in competition ploughing, the mouldboards are long with a gentle turn. The round disc is the coulter, which cuts into the soil parting from the furrow to be lifted from the remainder of the soil. The spoked wheel transports the plough and also drives the mechanism to lift the plough out of work when a rope is pulled by the driver. Both the main wheel and the rear wheel can be adjusted to control the working depth of the plough. The big trailing chains guide straw into the bottom of the furrow where it will be buried. The smaller chains are towing 'boats' to apply an extra polish to the finished furrows.

Above right: This man-killer was Fowler's answer to mechanical ploughing. It was controlled by the operator walking behind, with the two furrows being ploughed in front of him. These motor ploughs put up a good performance, probably benefiting from weight transfer from the plough to the drive wheels. In work cleats or spuds would be bolted to the wheels for extra grip.

Right: The extra ploughing needed during World War 2 required more tractors and more ploughs. Many of the tractors were Fordsons, while the Cockshutt plough from Canada was imported by R. A. Lister and sold as the Lister Cockshutt. While it was claimed that a Land Rover such as the one alongside could pull a two-furrow plough, this was rarely done in practice.

main work with the horse teams still finishing off each field.

By the 1930s the typical tractor plough had been established as either a two- or three-furrow plough, trailed from a fixed drawbar on the tractor. There would be plenty of provision to adjust this drawbar to suit a particular tractor. Adjustments could be made on the move by two controls, shaped like starting handles, while the mechanical trip was virtually universal. Out of work the plough would travel short distances on two transport wheels, with usually a tail wheel. Trailer ploughs still used today for competitions may well carry other modifications added by the owner, which make them appear even more complicated.

While plough design was being refined, many

farmers were finding it unprofitable to plough so much of their land. In the 1920s and 1930s, to offset falling prices, men were sacked and areas under the plough declined. The main customers for tractor ploughs were progressive farmers willing to risk taking on more land at low rents, which they could farm cheaply.

The next step in plough design was the introduction of the Ferguson Brown tractor, the first practical combination of engine and plough in a single unit. Motor ploughs had previously enjoyed a short period of popularity but had not been a commercial success. Sales of the Ferguson Brown tractor were likewise disappointing, but it did demonstrate that a tractor with a mounted plough could get into areas that a trailer plough had to miss. For the driver a light touch on a lever offered power to lift the plough clear of the soil, which was particularly appreciated if the plough became clogged with trash. However, the hydraulics functioned only when the tractor was in gear and moving, which meant that lifting the plough had to be completed before an obstruction was met. Today this seems inconvenient, but at the time it was regarded as no more difficult than ensuring that the plough trip on a trailer plough had functioned.

With the outbreak of World War 2, demand for any type of plough increased immediately. Neglected grassland was being brought back into cultivation as rapidly as possible, being urgently needed to grow more crops. Some of this ground contained hidden obstacles and tree roots, so many trailer ploughs were supplied with some form of weak link to prevent damage to the plough, causing it to detach itself from the tractor. There were two snags to this excellent idea. If the plough had a trip rope and it was tied to the driver's arm, it would hold the driver back as the tractor carried on, resulting in a startled driver sitting on the ground watching his or her departing tractor (the wartime emergency meant that many women unexpectedly found themselves promoted to ploughmen). The temptation was for drivers to override the breakaway device, but then the ploughs would suffer damage when they were dragged through sturdy tree roots. This led to the importation of specialised 'stump jump' ploughs as used in Australia. Instead of detaching from the tractor, the share concerned merely bent back, rose up over the obstacle and reset itself to carry on ploughing. Fifty years later, with modern ploughs, most makers fit some form of breakaway to release a plough body that hits an immovable object.

Below: The introduction of the Ferguson mounted plough eliminated the need for a drawbar and depth control wheels. The plough could be raised and lowered by a light movement of the hydraulic control lever.

Right: A few Fordson tractors were even fitted with a three-point linkage conversion to take a mounted plough, and at least this one has been preserved.

Below: As the Ferguson patents ran out, other tractor-makes offered depth control, removing the need for a depth wheel. On this Ransomes' plough the rear wheel was retained and made hydraulically operated. In the background is an Oliver plough attached to an Allis Chalmers B-type tractor.

Disc ploughs were also tried. Instead of shares, large discs were dragged at an angle in a frame, which produced an effect similar to ploughing. Later, the same effect would be produced by the so-called heavy-duty disc harrows.

Heavy ploughs were widely used behind crawler tractors for land reclamation and to cover large areas of ground under wet conditions.

A number of imported Ford Ferguson tractors demonstrated that these small machines with a plough attached could operate under some extremely difficult conditions. Since the hydraulics were designed to dump all lift if the plough hit an obstacle, they were unexpectedly effective when ploughing root-infested ground. They earned a good reputation, which proved useful when Harry Ferguson started tractor production after the war.

The postwar period was marked by the spread of tractors fitted with three-point linkage. Rubery Owen started manufacturing ploughs for the Ferguson company to sell, and Ford started manufacture of a mounted plough at a plant that had previously made components for Bren-gun carriers. Other manufacturers also felt that they should introduce mounted versions of the ploughs they were offering, or enter this field. In the next chapter we can take a closer look at three-point linkages.

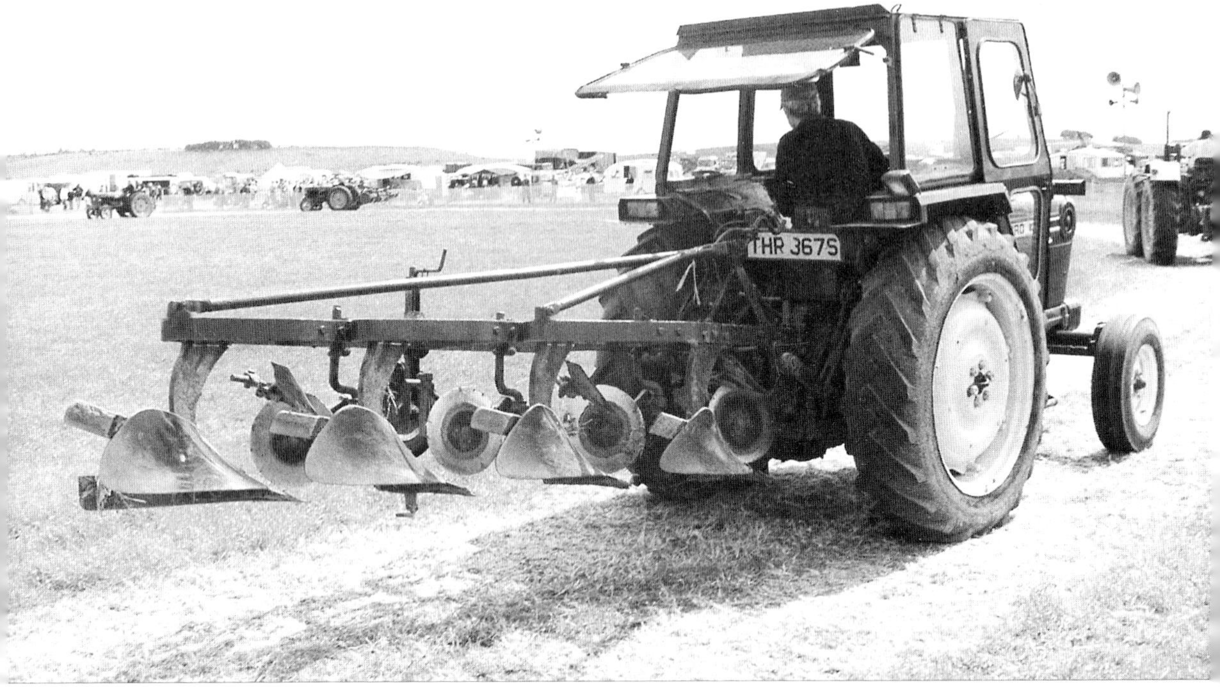
THR 367S

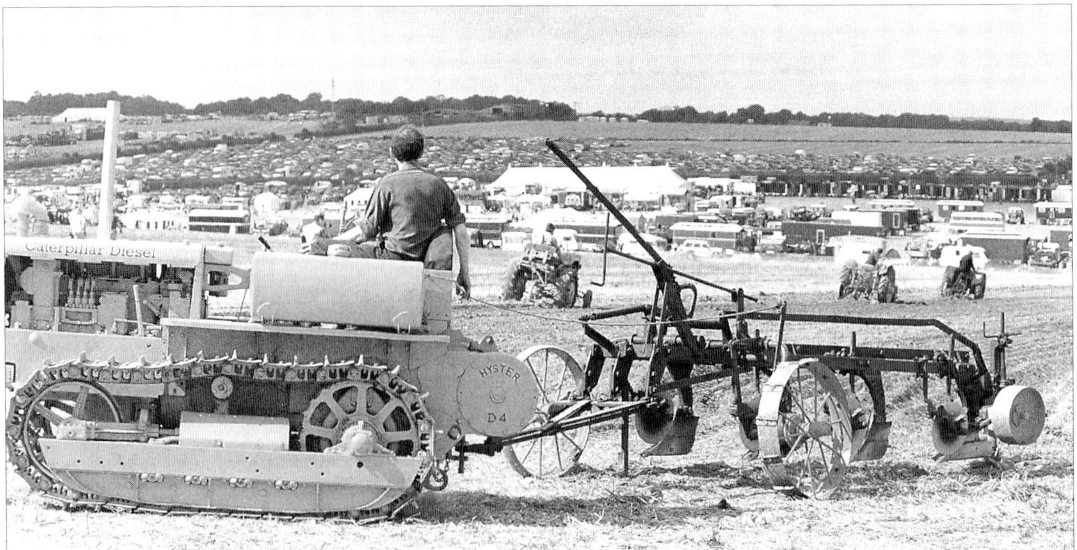
Caterpillar Diesel
HYSTER
D4

Above: A reversible plough carries two sets of plough bodies, and by adjusting their relative position it can be made to plough to either left or right. Ferguson's single-furrow reversible was particularly useful in cramped spaces like market gardens.

Top left: To avoid conflict with Ferguson patents, not all tractors were fitted with depth control. To cope, some designs of mounted plough were fitted with an adjustable depth wheel even though the plough could be lifted for transport.

Bottom left: Since a plough throws furrows to one side, it can only work with unploughed ground to its left. Time is wasted as it has to travel along the headland out of work to be in a position to return doing more useful work, wasting time and leaving uneven ridges and furrows at intervals across the field. Note that if a plough was to be pulled by a crawler, as here, extra strength in construction was needed.

Because they could only work at full depth when ploughing into an existing furrow, conventional ploughs left ridges and furrows at intervals across a field, which was a nuisance during later cultivation. In the 1960s it began to be realised that bigger tractors and bigger ploughs were wasting a lot of time turning round and travelling on headlands. Reversible or 'one-way' ploughs had always been built in small numbers - even horse-drawn versions had been offered. However, a mounted plough that was able to turn over and plough in the opposite direction enabled a tractor to turn back the way it had just come. Ploughing could now start from one side of the field. A one-way plough also left a more level field, which reduced jolting for sprayers and fertiliser-spreaders, helping accuracy.

As reversible ploughs grew heavier there came a point at which they became too heavy for some tractors to lift them clear of the ground. Even with front ballast, tractors became unstable. To overcome this, semi-mounted ploughs were introduced with a sturdy tail wheel, which could be raised and lowered hydraulically so that the plough could be supported at both ends when it was out of work.

Conversely, the increasing size of tractors meant that bigger ploughs with more furrows were needed to provide a suitable load for the tractor. In turn these bigger ploughs had to become more sophisticated, and this trend still continues.

Another parallel trend was to avoid ploughing altogether. This was variously described as the 'direct drilling', 'no till' or 'low till' system. In dry parts of the world this conserved moisture, giving the prospect of a better crop in a dry year. A compromise adopted by some users was to plough shallower furrows, which required more furrows on the plough and produced an implement somewhere

Below: **David Brown added reversible ploughs to its range in 1969. With an abrupt twist on the mouldboard, the plough produced a broken furrow. It was turned over manually by a strong pull on the operating lever at the front.** *RLM*

Above: With the Opico Square Plough the square bulldozer-type blades could be swung at an angle to the tractor's direction of travel. By altering the angle it could be made to plough to either side.

Below: The Howard Paraplow was not designed to invert a furrow in the normal way but to lift and loosen compacted soil. While it needed a powerful tractor, it could achieve many of the benefits of ploughing, but to a greater depth. (The wheels are a separate purchase from the same farm sale.)

Left: Some soils are particularly sticky, and to reduce build-up the slatted mouldboard was introduced. The separate miniature mouldboards are skims that plough a small mini-furrow, which drops into the bottom of the main furrow to be buried. A product of the German maker Lemken, bigger ploughs like this were introduced to match more powerful tractors.

Centre left: Occasionally a forgotten idea gets rediscovered. The furrow press was designed to follow immediately behind a plough to firm down the furrows and break down large lumps. Under the right conditions it was an effective first stage to producing a tilth.

Below: Stubble is being ploughed with the intention of drilling cereals soon after. The furrow press is breaking up the soil sufficiently for sowing to be achieved by a combination of a power harrow and seed drill.

between a plough and a cultivator. Other experiments were carried out with the shape of the plough body, particularly those types affected by the increased speed at which tractor and plough outfits were travelling.

Unusual designs and shapes of mouldboard were tried. Higher forward speeds meant that more gentle curves would produce the same finished furrow. Some soil types are particularly difficult to plough because they stick to the plough body, so slatted mouldboards were employed to reduce friction and sticking. Only 60 years ago farmers working soil with a high clay content were still using ploughs with wooden mouldboards for the same reason.

As well as experiments in different plough body design, manufacturers were looking at stresses within the plough itself and trying to come up with simplified designs. Later, computer-aided design was used to measure the stresses more accurately, enabling the design of light, strong structures to resist them.

Today's ploughs are a far cry from the blacksmith-made implements that started the last century. Now they have to cope with the large amount of straw that needs to be ploughed in under some systems - to reduce blockages, clearances between bodies and under the frame have been increased - while with powerful four-wheel-drive tractors there has been a revival of the old practice of attaching a furrow press to improve the effect of the ploughing. Widths of individual furrows have been increased, and adjustments can be made from the driver's seat on the move. The latest ploughs have a fairly sophisticated electro-hydraulic system, so that several functions are performed in order as the plough comes out of work. Always the objective is to enable the ploughman to get more work done in the time available.

Above: With plenty of power available this John Deere is pulling not only a seven-furrow reversible Kevernland plough but also a furrow press.

Left: This JCB Fastrac is pulling a five-furrow Rabe reversible plough in Devon. High-speed tractors allow a contractor or farmer to use the same plough in fields scattered over a wide area. One outfit like this can do the work of two slightly smaller tractors based at different locations. This is likely to be the pattern of commercial farming in the future.

5. The Three-point Linkage: A Simple Yet Revolutionary Idea

One of the biggest technical developments to affect implement-makers was the introduction of an entirely new way of coupling implements to tractors. Harry Ferguson and his team came up with an idea that totally transformed tractor design. Ferguson had noticed that a tractor pulling a separate implement was not very efficient; under wet conditions the tractor's drive wheels would slip while the implement dug in. He reasoned that if the implement was attached to the tractor, the weight that caused the implement to sink in could be doing a useful job imposing extra weight on the tractor's rear wheels. As a bonus, the forces generated tended to hold the front wheels down, stopping the tractor from rearing.

Even before Ferguson's work we see with hindsight that there had been clues to the advantages of weight transfer. The Fowler motor plough and others of the same type performed surprisingly well under difficult conditions. At least one example of the Ideal tractor was produced in Staffordshire around the end of World War 1; it was pictured with a form of mounted plough but other details are scanty.

After various trials it was found that what we now know as the three-point linkage was the most effective way of coupling implement and tractor. To operate this Ferguson used what in the 1930s was a fairly uncommon technology, hydraulics. From the driver's point of view a light touch on the control lever meant that the implement rose or fell effortlessly. Compared with hauling on levers, tugging on ropes, or frantically winding handles or control wheels, this was delightfully easy.

For an implement manufacturer the arrival of the three-point linkage was a very different story. Here was a tractor manufacturer that proposed to sell both tractors and implements. If it sold its tractors in the numbers it was anticipating, an awful lot of farmers would not want the present design of implements, as mounted implements needed to be light but strong. Ferguson System implements had no need of depth wheels, as the working depth could be set from the tractor seat.

Left: This mounted harrow demonstrates the flexibility of the three-point linkage system. Moving harrows used to be an awkward job, but now, attached to a framework, they could be transported from field to field. Once in the field with the framework lowered and folded out, a considerable area could be harrowed in one pass by the tractor. Yet by detaching three simple connections the harrow could be left and the tractor released for another job.

Top left: Another type of harrow, shown partly opened. Although the frame is rigid, the individual harrows are still free to follow their own path attached only by chains.

Centre left: The posthole digger was a great labour-saver when erecting fences. The drive shaft has been removed for safety, but it was driven by the tractor's power take-off (PTO). In suitable soil conditions it saved much handwork putting up fence posts.

Bottom left: The Ferguson fertiliser spinner was a simple and effective method of applying fertiliser. The spinning disc was driven from the tractor PTO, and because it was mounted on a three-point linkage, the spinner left no wheel marks except those of the tractor itself. With a hopper full of fertiliser it was quite possible to treat a small paddock with one trip from the farm to the field. While the spinner could be quickly detached, it was important that it was thoroughly cleaned before it was left, otherwise fertiliser would corrode the machine. The tractor is a Ferguson 35, which had a rather more sophisticated hydraulic system than the previous Ferguson 20, and it is in the short-lived bronze and grey livery.

Above and right: The Ferguson earth scoop was another great labour-saving device for farm construction projects. When lowered and the tractor driven forward it would scoop up the equivalent of two or three barrow-loads of earth, then, with the linkage lifted, the driver could transport it to where it was needed. With a pull on the handle the rear linkage folded to dump the load on the ground, all without the driver leaving his seat. What an improvement over pick, shovel and wheelbarrow! The upper tractor is a US-built Ford Ferguson while the Ferguson below was built in Coventry.

Right: The slurry scraper is a vital tool for any dairy farmer, but it has to be mounted to cope with the necessary manoeuvring. Used on smooth concrete it can move considerable quantities of semi-fluid dung from where it has been deposited by livestock to where it can be stored. The 'scraper tractor' is usually the final relegation for the oldest tractor on the farm, and many tractors now preserved will have had a spell on this job.

Below and bottom: Even trailed machines could benefit from three-point linkage. This Ferguson seed drill is firmly attached to the link arms, and the action of lowering them puts the drill into work and starts the drive mechanism. Since the drill is intended for one-man operation, a gap is provided between the seed dispenser and the tube. Any blockage in the tube will soon cause grain to spill out to be noticed from the tractor seat. Altering the position and size of the various gears alters the sowing rate as required.

Other makers offering mounted implements soon realised that a Ferguson dealer would give priority to the Ferguson implements that came from the same source as the tractors. Both David Brown and the Fordson Major introduced the option of three-point linkage, as did the new Nuffield, but all three manufacturers offered a range of 'approved' implements to suit their own tractors. To start with, the Ferguson tractor and the previous Ford Ferguson could use the same implements. The Nuffield and Fordson implements were virtually interchangeable, but they needed depth wheels. When an effort was made to standardise dimensions the Ferguson became 'Category One' and the other two 'Category Two'. David Brown's linkage had minor differences again. Happily, with the introduction of the Massey Ferguson 65, clever linkage design meant that tractors could take either category of implements, and certain of the implements were fitted with special linkage pins to allow operation by either category.

Coupling up was always made to look easy by demonstrators, but in the real world it was often necessary to manhandle the implements to align them for coupling, which was acceptable with relatively light and clean implements. Inventors and

Above: The Ferguson potato planter also made good use of the three-point linkage. Based on the standard tool bar, the potato tubers are carried in the sheet steel hopper above, and two seats are provided for operators. When the ridging bodies are lowered they form a ridge to bury the potato tubers, which are dropped through a tube just in front of the ridger bodies.

Below: Accurate spacing in the furrows is ensured by the ingenious bell mechanism behind the ridger. The bell striker could be operated by various concentric circles of dimples on the wheel. By choosing a different circle the effective spacing of seed was altered. As far as the operator is concerned, all that has to be done is to drop one potato each time the bell rings, although after only a few minutes this becomes a dull and automatic routine.

Above: Once Ferguson had demonstrated the possibilities of the three-point linkage, other makers were quick to follow. Nuffield tractors offered three-point linkage from their introduction, although it was an option at extra cost, and patent restrictions meant that, unlike the Ferguson System, implements had to be fitted with a depth control wheel. Due to the size of the Nuffield, the designers opted to make their linkage broadly compatible with that being fitted to the Fordson Major E27N; in time this was standardised as 'Category Two' linkage. One sensible Nuffield feature was a mechanical latch that could be set to lock the linkage in the up position. When travelling, the lock reduced the risk of the implement dropping and being damaged. Early Nuffields could generate only 1,000psi hydraulic pressure, which would prove insufficient to operate some implements with remote rams such as tipping trailers.

Right: Professional demonstrators position their tractors so accurately that coupling or uncoupling an implement is a quick, effortless job, although even they have to dismount to fit the pins and clips. The rest of us usually need some help to heave the implement slightly to get it to match up. By fitting a triangular A-frame to the tractor's three-point linkage, the driver can plug it into any implement fitted with a matching triangular socket. Once plugged in, the implement is firmly coupled without the driver having to leave his seat, and uncoupling is just as quick. Teagle of Truro still manufacture these and have made the job of coupling and uncoupling much easier for users. *Courtesy Teagle of Truro*

manufacturers offered various improvements to make coupling easier, most involving either a rigid frame or some form of hook or adjustable coupling to speed the job and reduce the effort.

Now that tractors had a built-in hydraulic supply, designers started to exploit this power source. Loads could be lifted without effort. Mounted transport boxes offered ground-level loading. A buckrake could be backed under fodder or bales and used to lift and transport the load. Others reasoned that they could use the linkage to lift lighter loads to a greater height. Indeed, if hydraulic pressure was on tap, why not feed it into other hydraulic rams to produce loaders or diggers, or to adjust the arms of a hedge-cutter or the pick-up reel of an implement? As a result, various designers kept adding more uses to a tractor with hydraulic

Above: With hydraulic linkage it was easy to pick up and transport a machine, and hydraulic power was also on tap to operate a digging machine. A slew loader like this by McConnell could dig trenches, load manure or load sugar beet when fitted with an appropriate bucket. It was built primarily for agricultural use, but later designs for industrial use needed purpose-built subframes or even specialised tractors. As they became bigger the makers sometimes found it worth offering the option of a PTO-driven pump for improved performance.

linkage. This did much to ensure that independent implement-makers were kept busy.

Crawler tractors continued to use a simple pin hitch, which the makers argued was sufficient for trailer ploughs. However, a number of firms felt that a form of three-point hitch would be useful. The way a crawler steers means that the back end moves sideways when turning, so this had to be allowed for. The answer proved to be a form of three-point linkage that could swing in relation to the tractor. As with wheeled tractors, a crawler with a

Above: This Bomford hedge-trimmer is carried on the three-point linkage, and the rotating flail that cuts the hedge is hydraulically driven. The power needed to drive the flail means that there is an additional hydraulic pump included, driven off the tractor PTO. Additional valves regulate the hydraulic rams that control the arm.

Right: By fitting a hammer mill with three-point linkage mounting pins an awkward lump of machinery could be made mobile, and the tractor also used to provide the power. As a result, a high-output mill could be used at several locations in turn to prepare grain as animal feed. A mill like this would need an operator to feed in the grain and bag off the feed. Today, where farms mill their own grain, much smaller electrically driven hammer mills run unattended, making big mills like this obsolete.

61

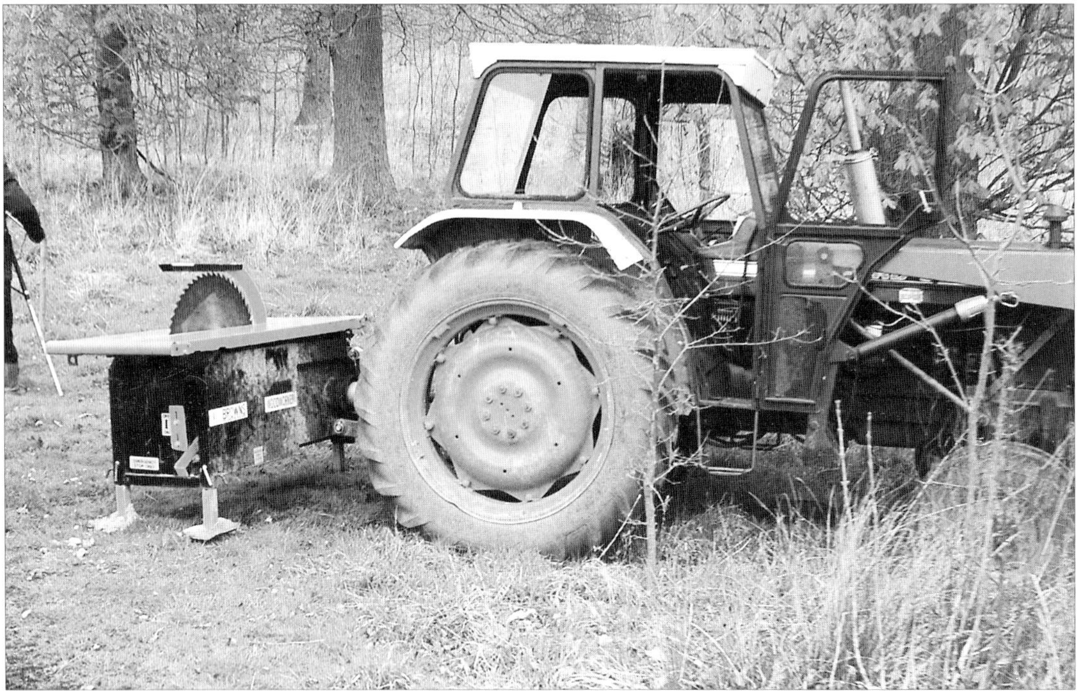

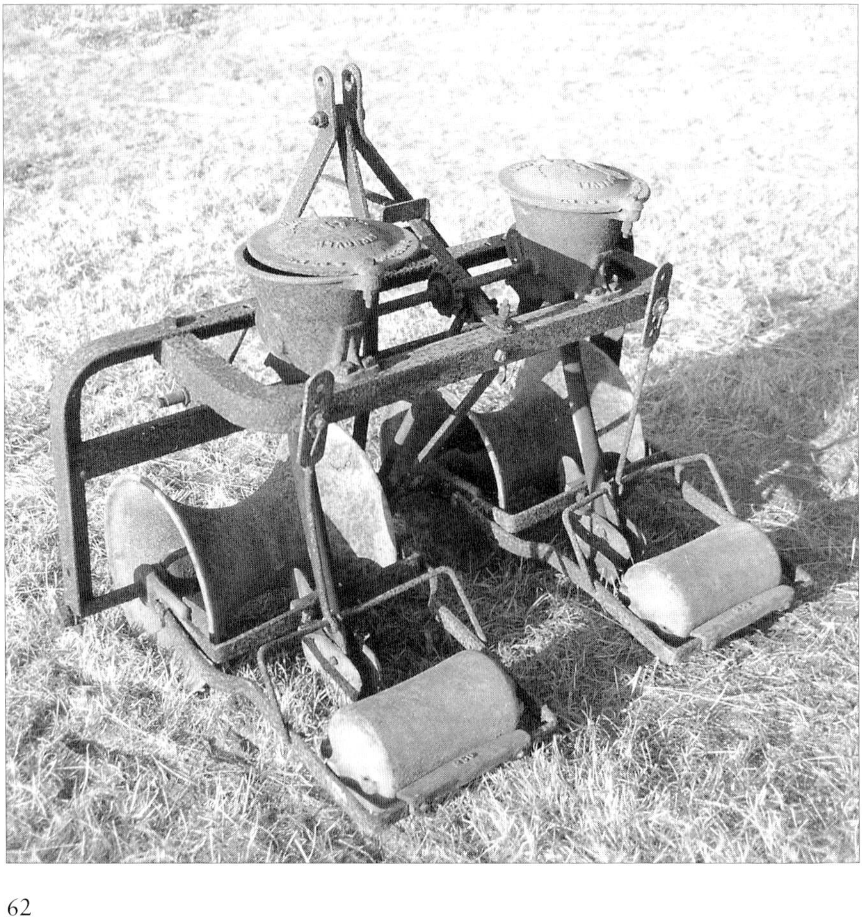

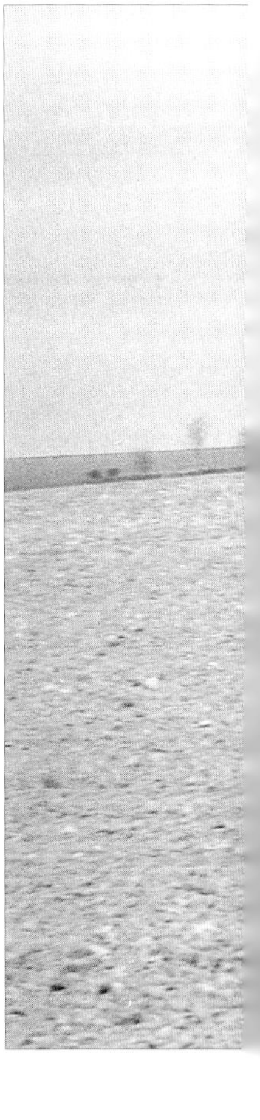

linkage was better able to manoeuvre and needed less effort from the driver. At first three-point linkages were offered as conversions, but later crawler manufacturers added them as a regular option.

The three-point linkage did have disadvantages, and some drivers still preferred to use just a single hitch-pin to couple a trailed implement. A mounted implement out of work could make a tractor very light to steer or even cause it to rear. On sloping ground a lifted implement could make the tractor unstable, although often this was on a slope too steep even to consider using a trailed implement.

As projecting implements, ploughs in particular, became longer they became dangerous in traffic as they swung out, blocking the road as the tractor turned. The three-point linkage had to be scaled up as the tractors increased in size, and designers had to give more consideration to the problem of implements swinging on turns. One answer was the semi-mounted arrangement with a wheel or two at the rear to support part of the weight.

Left: A sawbench is another awkward machine made portable by use of the three-point linkage. Once fitted to the tractor it can be taken to the woods, and timber can be cut up for firewood with the minimum of manhandling. Note that even when correctly guarded, as here, it can be dangerous to distract an operator using a saw.

Below left: Although a tractor with three-point linkage was supposed to require special implements, a local craftsman or blacksmith was sometimes able and willing to modify an existing implement. This horse-drawn root drill has been fitted with mounting points to extend its useful life.

Below: As tractors grew in size the lifting capacity of the three-point linkage kept pace. Since the tractor could handle heavier weights, mounted implements could be made with a greater working width. Here, by using a relatively narrow seed hopper, only the tines need to be folded when travelling.

6. Cultivation: Preparing the Soil

Above: A set of locally made wooden harrows with tines big enough to be a light cultivator. The individual tines passed down through the frame and were retained by plates fixed to the top of the frame.

Once the land has been ploughed, further preparation of the soil is needed before most crops can be sown. The aim is to prepare a suitable tilth - that is to get the soil in the best condition to take the chosen seed for growing. Weather, urgency and soil types sometimes mean that less than ideal conditions have to be accepted.

At first sight farmers are faced with a bewildering choice of different implements to produce the necessary tilth. To some extent the choice of implement is a matter of personal experience of the land being farmed, and it can also be affected by the farmer's own opinion as to the type of tilth he requires.

When local manufacturers made implements, one might enjoy an excellent reputation in one part of the country yet be virtually unknown elsewhere.

Today implements are marketed over much wider areas. Many countries may be supplied from the same manufacturing plant, so they now tend to be better known and much more heavily advertised.

The first family of implements to produce a tilth was the fixed-tine cultivator. This has a number of tines that are drawn through and penetrate the soil with a lifting and battering action. For initial cultivations the implements work relatively deep and require a fair amount of power to pull them through the soil. Soil can be abrasive, so the parts most affected by wear need to be readily replaceable

Left: Seen here is a typical blacksmith conversion of a horse-drawn cultivator for operation behind a tractor with three-point linkage, although, unlike a proper Ferguson implement, there is no weight transfer. Many implements took on a second lease of life after the arrival of a tractor. One big advantage of a conversion like this was that it made it is easy to lift the cultivator clear of the ground, allowing any rubbish or trash that had built up to drop clear.

Centre left: Steam ploughing sets needed cultivators of massive construction to withstand the strains that could be imposed by tackling baked clay ground at considerable depth.

Bottom: Less power was available to pull early mounted cultivators. They were not even expected to work to the same depth. As a result they were much less costly to manufacture.

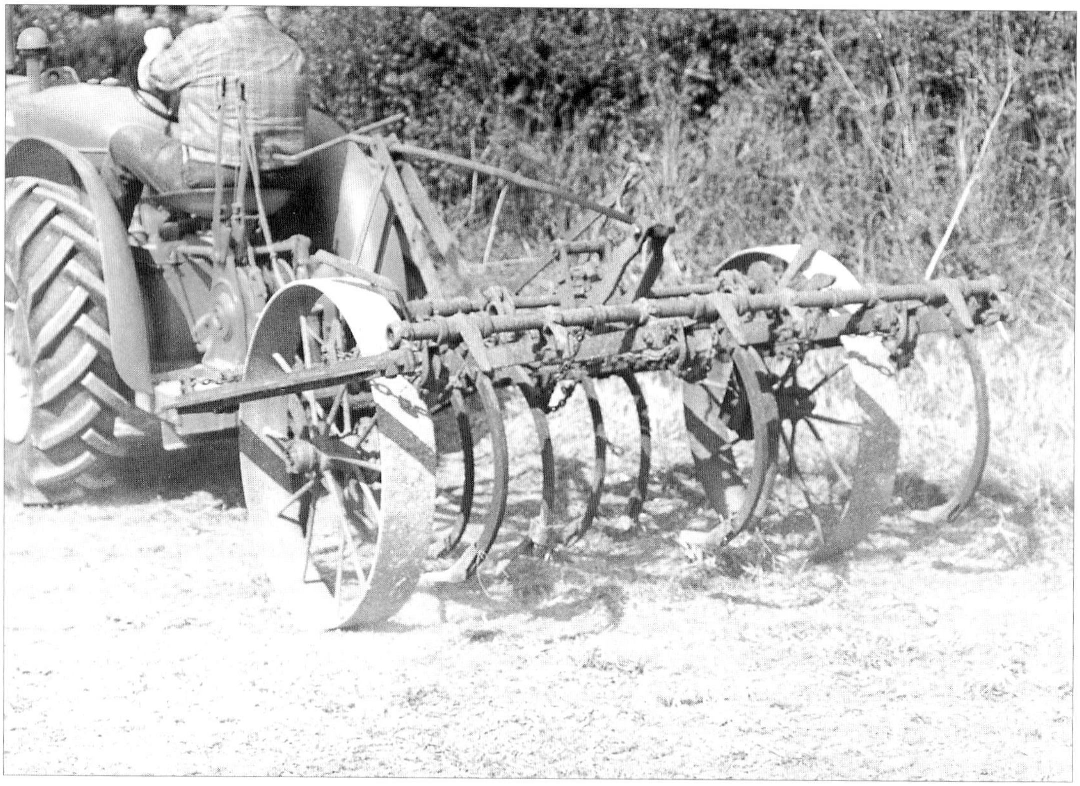

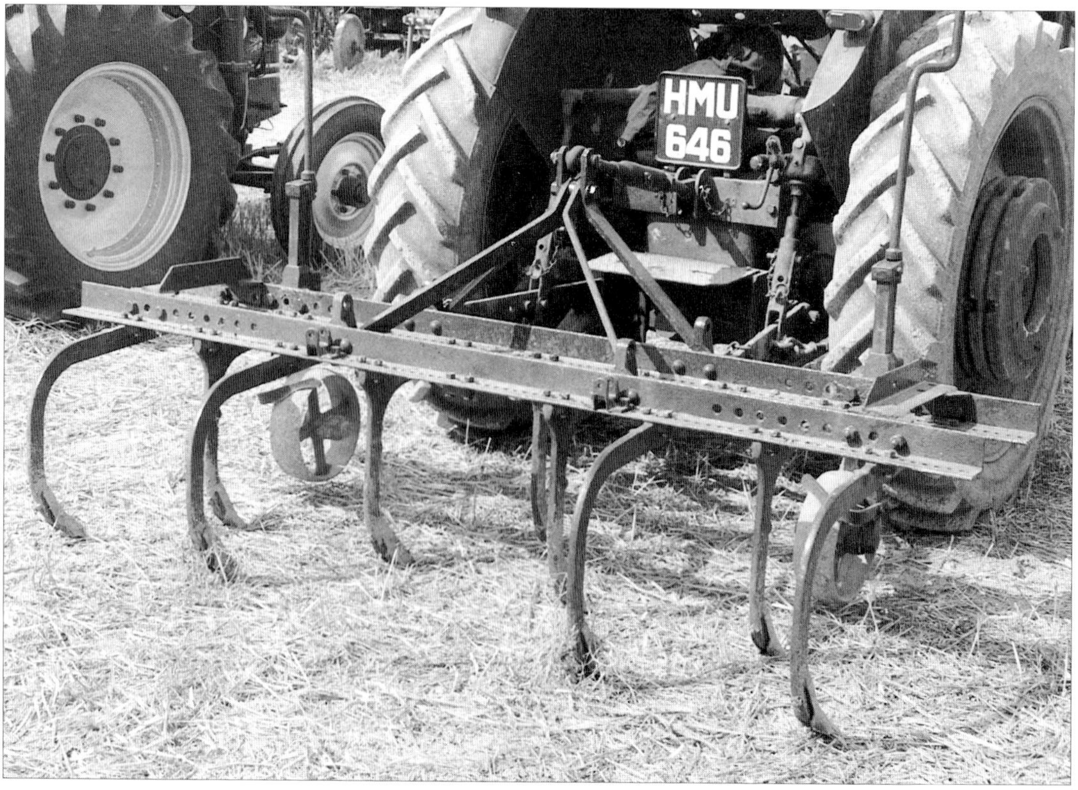
HMU
646

Top left: By allowing the legs to swing, yet restrained by chains, this Ransomes cultivator imparts extra movement to the soil, which tends to bring weeds to the surface.

Bottom left: The Ransomes cultivator shown on the previous page in close-up. Despite its lighter construction, in work it was still capable of doing a good job.

Above: Easy going in heavily cultivated ground allows this cultivator to go down deep without overloading the Fordson Major, which was supplied without any form of hydraulic linkage.

Right: Ferguson also offered a mounted tool bar. Here the cultivator is equipped with two different types of tines.

ploughing contractor, if available. A massive cultivator would replace the plough and could work deep even on hard-baked soil. While this saved the horses at the time, the big lumps left behind could make it hard going for them afterwards.

When tractors replaced horses the cultivator became a trailed, wheeled implement. Some form of screw adjustment was included, which, by changing the relative position of the wheels and the tines, set the working depth of the cultivator. A sturdy frame took clamps or other attachments to fix the legs that actually did the cultivating.

This flexibility of design enabled the cultivator to be built up to different specifications according to

when worn. Further passes, perhaps travelling in a different direction, will have the effect of continuing to reduce the average size of the lumps of soil. The working width and depth of the cultivator affects the amount of power needed; early horse-drawn cultivators had relatively few legs, but still required several horses to pull them.

For really deep cultivation beyond the capacity of his horses, a farmer might have used a steam

FARMALL
33
CAJ 246

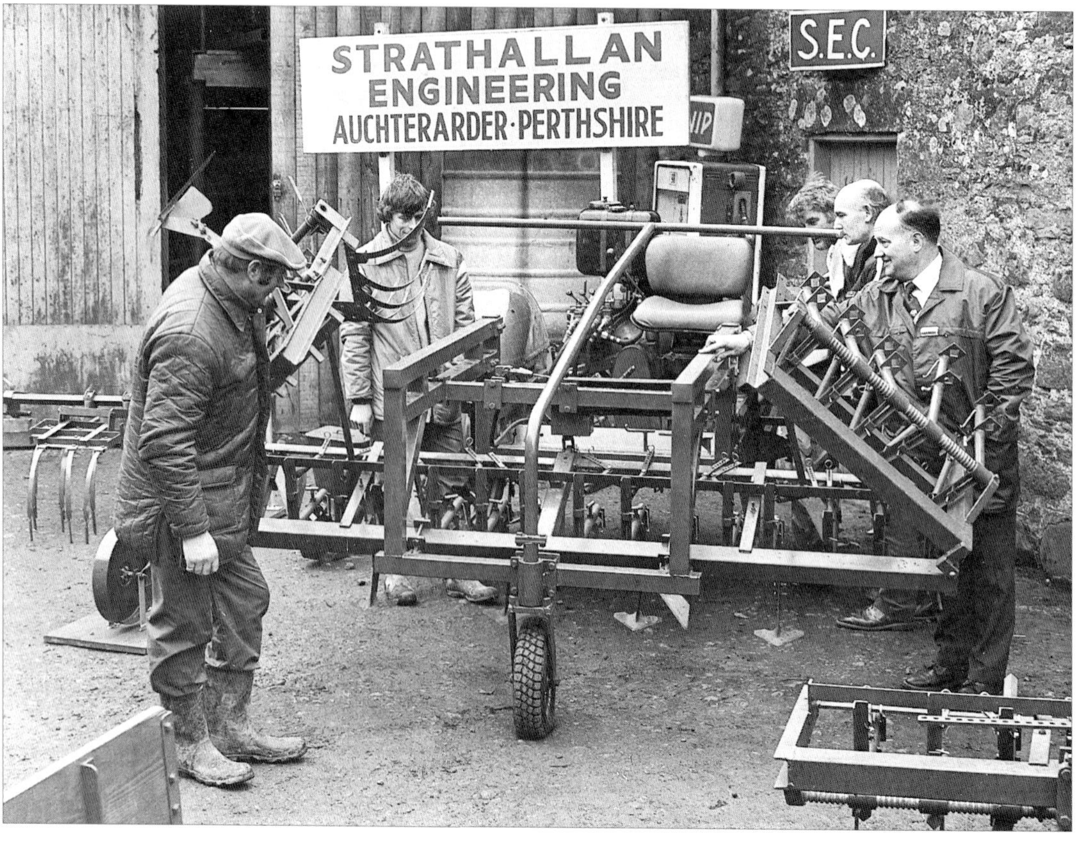
STRATHALLAN
ENGINEERING
AUCHTERARDER·PERTHSHIRE
S.E.C.

Top left: World War 2 meant that there was an increased demand for potatoes, and specialised imported tractors like this Farmall A had enough clearance to fit a tool bar beneath. By varying the parts fitted to the tool bar it could be used for cultivating, hoeing or ridging, as required. Mounting the tool bar was made much simpler by the tractor-maker, which provided suitable mounting points as part of the basic design.

Bottom left: The Bean tool carrier was introduced in the 1940s but, intended only for inter-row hoeing, sales petered out. However, Mike Norton (far right) of Strathallan Engineering later revived the design, updating it with a diesel engine and hydraulic system and a rather more comfortable seat. Steering was still by the crude but effective tiller, which was light and precise in action. *RLM*

Top right: The more flexible spring-tine cultivator has been around longer than most people realise, and was originally offered as a horse-drawn implement.

Centre right: For this Ferguson cultivator the tool bar has been specified with sprung legs. Under very heavy conditions the legs can break back rather than suffer damage.

Bottom right: This spring-tine cultivator is a purpose-built mounted implement, which on small plots can be lifted to reverse right into the corners. Note that the tractor is fitted with easily detachable extension cage wheels, which increase the overall width of the tractor's rear wheels and, by spreading the load, prevent the tractor from sinking into the ground and leaving ruts.

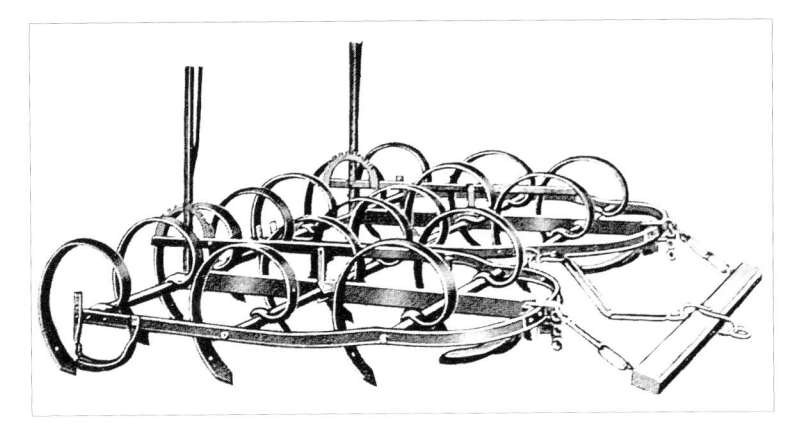

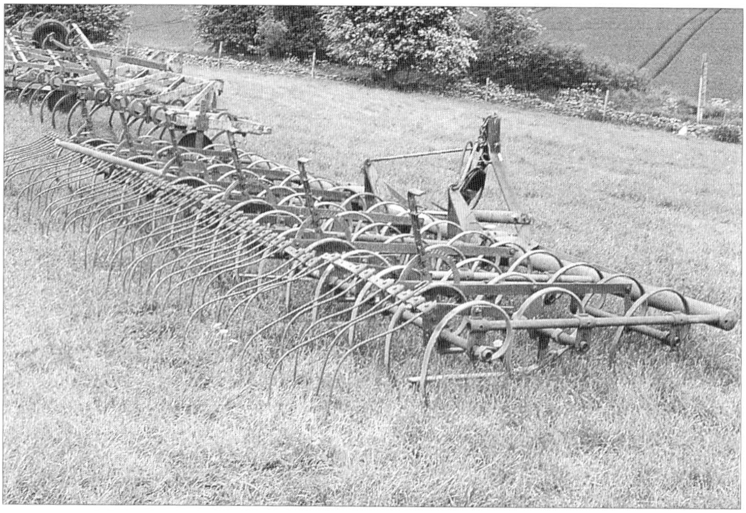

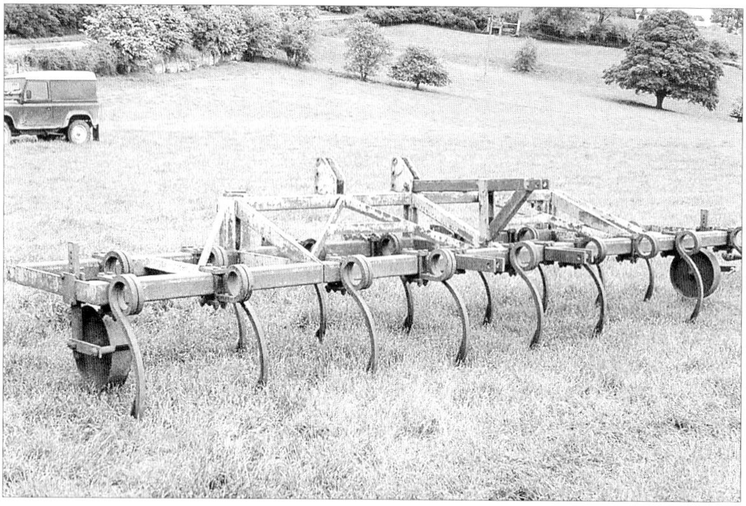

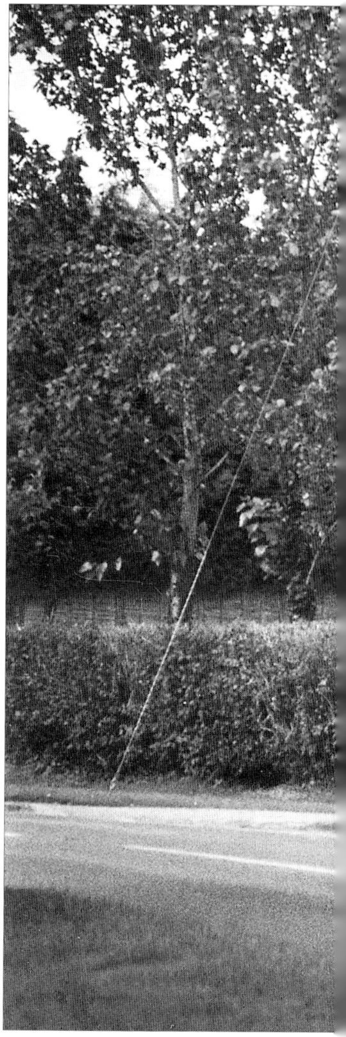

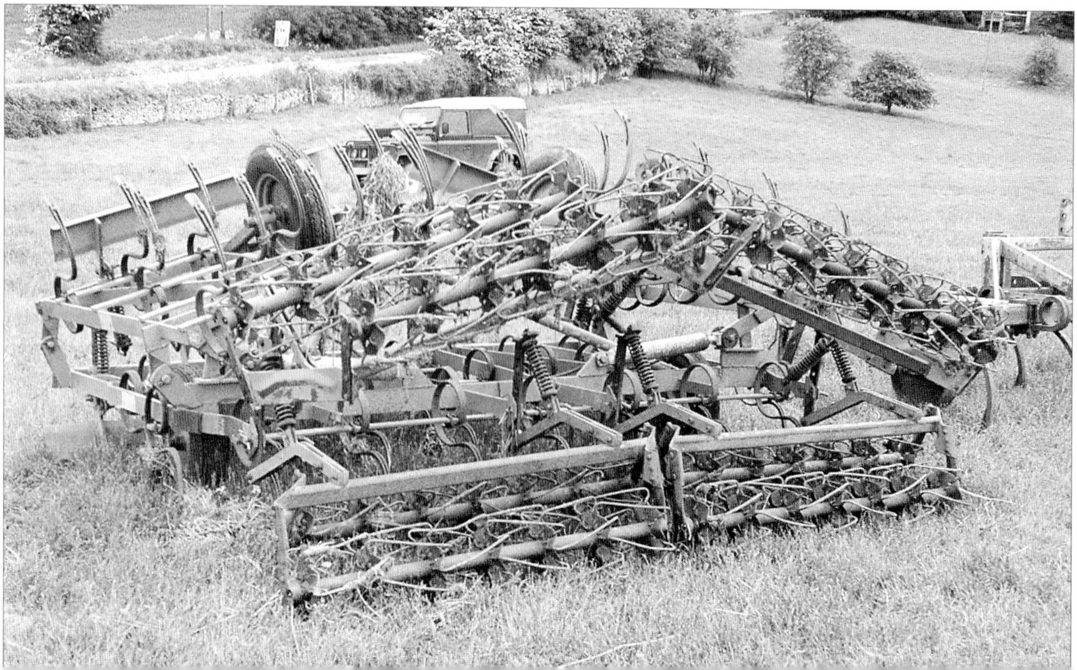

Top left: Spring-tine cultivators can be built in a variety of widths according to the power of the tractor being used. One advantage of this design is that it imparts a vibrating action to the tines as they pass through the soil, which means that clods are struck more vigorously and broken up more effectively. The tines also have a very effective weeding action, pulling roots and broken trash to the surface. Extra power giving higher speed would make it even more effective.

Centre left: Another variation is the 'pigtail' cultivator, where the legs themselves are made with a couple of turns so there is some flexibility if they strike an obstacle. As you can see from the construction of the beams, this is a much more solid type of cultivator and needs a more powerful tractor to operate it.

Left: As cultivators have increased in width there has arisen the problem of getting them through gateways and travelling down narrow roads. A simple and effective answer is to design a cultivator that can fold. Almost concealed within the frame of this cultivator are two double-acting hydraulic rams, which fold the outer wings upwards and inwards. Folding is made more complicated by the open-frame rollers that follow behind the cultivator to provide a further levelling and crumbling action.

Above: When folded, a modern mounted cultivator can travel quite easily on the road, yet when unfolded it can provide sufficient load to require a powerful tractor.

the requirements of a particular customer. In practice, once the design had been settled on it was rarely altered in use. Few farmers could face the delay of major reconstruction of an implement just when conditions were ideal to get on with field work.

To save the stresses and strains of dragging the cultivator round at the headland, some form of trip mechanism was fitted whereby the cultivator could be lifted clear of the soil and trailed round before being tripped again to start work.

As tractors increased in size, makers began to offer different layouts of cultivator, and as the tines became more substantial, their working points got bigger. These points wear away over a period of use, the rate of wear depending on the type of soil being cultivated. Some designs of point were made reversible so that they could be detached and turned through 180° before being refitted to get a second life out of them. Because of the protection of the points the tines themselves endure relatively little wear, and it is very unusual to need to replace the tines as well as the points.

Spring-tine cultivators are rather different from those with rigid tines. Somewhere within the construction of the tine there is either a substantial leaf spring or a coil spring, which either lets the tine have a breakaway action or allows it to vibrate, so that each tine is constantly changing its relative speed compared to that of the tractor towing it. The action of the springs also has a considerable extra shattering effect on the soil hit by the tips of the cultivator. This type of cultivator has more tines in proportion to its working width, and often their spacing and action mean that the same piece of soil may be affected by two or more tines as they pass over.

Lighter cultivators and other implements with small tines that engage the soil are classified as harrows, although the distinction between a cultivator and a harrow is not rigidly defined. Harrows tend to be used later than the cultivator in preparing a tilth, while some would actually be used for covering the seed after a drill had applied it. Compared with a cultivator, a harrow of the same working width will have more tines, and they will probably be in more rows across the machine. When drawn through the soil at speed, an individual clod of soil is likely to be knocked from side to side as the harrow passes over it, thus increasing the breaking-up action, but only on the shallow top layer of soil.

Below: The Wilder Pitchpole was somewhere between a cultivator and a heavy harrow. The four tines on each shaft were able to rotate through 90° when a lever was pulled, allowing any accumulated rubbish caught up in the tines to detach itself and be left behind. This action was particularly useful for renovating pastureland. It was also used for pulling out the roots of couch grass, which are long and tenacious.

Left: A simple mounted harrow could achieve the same result by being lifted to clear any build-up of rubbish.

Below left: Dowdeswell is based in a part of Warwickshire notorious for its heavy clay, and the clods, if allowed to bake hard, take some dealing with. As a result, the firm made strong tackle. This disc harrow will keep a powerful tractor working hard while producing a useful tilth. The outer wings are in the travel position; the transport wheels are forced down hydraulically to keep the discs clear of the ground.

The first harrows were simple horse-drawn devices, made with spikes driven through wooden balks of timber to hold them in their correct relative position. Blacksmiths then worked out ways of building all-metal harrows, and later designers came up with methods of using components made in quantity, assembled to produce various types of harrow. Some types were made to be reversible so that by turning over the complete frame an alternative type of tine engaged with the soil to produce a different type of action.

One effect of harrowing was that the harrow would tangle with strands of root and vegetable matter in the soil and draw them along. This tended to separate them from the soil and left the roots exposed on the surface. If weather conditions were favourable they would quickly shrivel up in the sunshine and die without producing further growth. However, sometimes this trash would accumulate within the harrow and would eventually block its action. The only cure was to lift the harrow clear of the vegetable matter and clean the accumulation from the teeth. This was a laborious and aggravating job and often involved a certain amount of moving the horse or the tractor while the clearing process was going on.

Wilders of Reading introduced one answer with the Pitchpole harrow. The tines were on axles, but were firmly held in position by a catch; releasing this catch let the tines revolve on the axle, and with luck this would leave the accumulated rubbish behind and the harrow could resume work without stopping.

Repeated harrowing was a recognised method of controlling couch grass. This weed has long straggling roots and, when broken, the severed parts will grow into plants. Many farmers collected up the harrowed roots and carted them to a place in the field where they were burned in a smouldering couch bonfire.

The introduction of the mounted harrow proved popular. Without leaving the tractor seat the driver could lift the harrow clear of any accumulation of vegetation, allowing it to fall away; the harrow could then be dropped back into work in front of the pile.

Above: With a modern high-horsepower tractor like this Case International 7230, an option is to pull two implements at once. Here a Simba Roll is leading a set of heavy Pettit disc harrows. This outfit is working ploughed ground in Lincolnshire in 2001, yet, as we have seen, horse-drawn equivalents of both implements were around a century before. Even with four teams of horses the job would have taken much longer.

Although described as a type of harrow, the disc harrow is very different in action from the tined implement, and consists of a series of tempered steel discs able to rotate on bearings. With the axle shaft of the discs set at an angle of 90° to the direction of travel of the power unit, the discs simply roll on the soil and exert a cutting action on any clods that happen to fall beneath them. In use the discs are normally set at a specific angle in relation to the forward travel; they still rotate but they also have a lifting and moving action, which has the effect of shifting the soil slightly to one side. This, together with the cutting action, which is accentuated, tends to reduce the size of clod. The clod-breaking action is directly proportional to the forward speed of the discs.

Originally a horse-drawn implement, under the right conditions the discs could do a good job. However, disc harrows had two major disadvantages: they were difficult to move between jobs, as they teetered along on little iron transport wheels, and in work, if they ran over a wet spot, they would rapidly fill with mud and halt the tractor. There can be few more disheartening jobs than extricating the tractor and the discs. Cunning drivers used to attach a chain between the disc harrows and the tractor, which gave them a better chance of getting out.

Since the discs revolved, under dusty conditions frequent greasing of all the bearings was needed. These were often made of hardwood; if they were frequently greased they were little harder to pull than precision bearings, but were much more tolerant of dust and neglect.

For a period disc harrows went out of fashion. Modern disc harrows are usually mounted or semi-mounted, but of much heavier construction. Some are now made in very substantial sizes, and with plenty of ballast weight they can even operate on uncultivated soil, perhaps serving as an alternative to a light ploughing.

So far all the implements described are operated by being towed or pulled along, and their efficiency is directly related to the speed at which they travel and the depth at which they are operated. Indeed, most of them are recognisably descended from horse-drawn implements, and even behind a tractor their work rates are limited by the traction available; often it was wheel slip that imposed the limit.

Manufacturers therefore began to consider how to apply the power of the tractor engine directly to some form of mechanism that engaged with the soil. There had been steam-operated digging machines, but these tended to be little more than individual demonstration machines. Probably the pioneer of applying engine power to soil-engaging implements was Cliff Howard in Australia, who developed a rotary cultivator linked to a tractor of his own design and manufacture. While this was efficient, it did not catch on in commercial terms.

The next power-driven implement was the Fowler Gyrotiller of the 1930s, but this was more like a travelling earthquake than a cultivation implement! The intention of the designer was to replace a winch-drawn heavy plough or cultivator with a power-driven implement capable of working to a depth of up to 24in (600mm) when preparing the ground for sugar cane.

Left: **Nature can provide unexpected entertainment for tractor drivers. The antics of the seagulls following this disc harrow offer a totally different type of bird-watching experience. As the number of tractors at work in an area decreases, the flocks have become much bigger.**

Right: As tractors became more powerful it made sense to apply much of their power to driving an implement. This Lely Roterra has vertical spikes that rotate under power, producing a stirring action that breaks up the soil, then any clods on the surface are crushed by the roller behind. The tractor is a Lely Hydro, with the reversible driving controls facing to the rear. The drawing on the display shows the thinking behind this innovative tractor, but while the tractor was short-lived, the implement proved a classic. *RLM*

Below right: This Fowler Gyrotiller is very securely attached to the firm's crawler tractor. The legs rotate as the tractor moves forward, and are able to work to a considerable depth, shattering and loosening the soil rather than inverting it. The machine was originally designed for preparing ground for sugar cane, and was later found to be ideal for reclaiming overgrown scrubland.

Left: While cultivating, many a tractor driver has recognised that the tractor wheels do an effective job in crushing clods. Ritchie Engineering came up with this simple and effective way of making the most of this action. These four pneumatic-tyred wheels were transported on the front linkage and, when lowered, provided sufficient weight to roll the clods in between the normal wheel tracks of the tractor. When lifted clear of the ground they acted as additional front weight to counterbalance an implement on the rear.

A few Gyrotillers remained in the United Kingdom. Used by contractors, they were not popular, as it was felt that they left the ground too loose, and it took a considerable period before it consolidated enough to support horses and tractors. However, during World War 2, when large areas of neglected land were being reclaimed, they proved useful tools for clearing overgrown scrubland. The rotors were extremely efficient in tearing up the underground roots of bushes and the like.

Meanwhile Howard had not lost interest in powered cultivation. He realised that the future lay in designing an implement that could be used by a tractor that was already on the farm. This would reduce the capital cost of changing to his powered cultivation system, known as Rotovation, and the saving would enable it to be more widely used.

The first version was offered as a conversion to fit the Fordson tractor and was driven from the belt pulley. In practice, the length of time needed to fit a Rotovator meant that the tractor became a dedicated cultivation machine.

Soon tractors were offered with the option of a power take-off (PTO), and fitting a power-driven implement, operated by the PTO shaft, became simpler. Also, with the implement either trailed behind or mounted on the three-point linkage, it would be much quicker to attach and detach it, leaving the tractor free for other jobs in the course of the year. For many years Howard Rotovator was the leading make of rotary cultivator, although other firms such as Fishleigh from Devon offered their own versions.

Early rotary machines offered a single fixed ratio between the speed of the power shaft and the cultivating shaft, and the efficiency of the cultivation mechanism could be affected by opening or shutting the rear shield of the cultivator, while altering the forward speed of the tractor by selecting a different gear ratio altered the number of chops in a set distance. The rotary cultivator was probably the only implement that didn't require to be pulled by a tractor - more often the tractor was trying to hold the cultivator back! Left to its own devices, the cultivator would act like a crude drive wheel and propel the tractor forward at a faster speed than was intended.

Later developments involved the addition of a set of drive gears within the power transmission, offering several different ratios between the PTO speed and the speed at which the cultivating shaft rotated. Newer tractors, with more gear ratios, offered yet more choice of forward speed to suit the type of soil and the type of tilth that was required.

Rotary cultivation marked a new step in the relationship between the implement and the tractor. Here was an implement that was capable of making use of and absorbing all the power that a tractor could produce. Indeed, smaller tractors were often left struggling to produce enough power to drive the implement at a satisfactory rate at the required forward speed. To overcome this Howard offered an auxiliary gearbox for use on Fergusons so that they could be geared down for a slower forward speed of travel. This permitted the Rotovator to work at a decent depth and width.

As patents ran out on the Rotovator design, other manufacturers entered the market with broadly

Above: Today, with fewer and stronger legs, a cultivator has become capable of doing much of the work of a plough, lifting and loosening the ground. With a roller on the back, the disturbed ground is levelled off and crumbled - effectively two jobs are done in one pass.

Left: Another combination implement is the Polymag. The front legs have a combined cultivating and hoeing action, then the topsoil is moved to both sides by the angled discs. Levelling with the crumbling roller produces an acceptable tilth in one or two passes.

similar machines. However, some manufacturers recalled that the original Gyrotiller worked with a vertical rotating spindle and tines, and this idea was revived with machines that had a series of vertical rotating clusters of tines that stirred their way through the soil. These proved extremely robust and again capable of absorbing all the power that was available.

A big advantage of power-driven rotary cultivators is that they can, to a certain extent, force a tilth even when conditions are not ideal. However, to do this under difficult conditions they have to be operated at slow forward speeds, so the work rate is slower than under better conditions. The PTO shaft absorbed more of the tractor's power than the wheels, which allowed them to be used under conditions where wheel grip could be difficult.

With conventional cultivation the soil could dry out too much, but by forcing a tilth in one pass there was relatively little loss of moisture from the soil, and seed could be planted in a moister seedbed, giving it a better chance of prompt growth. If it rained during sowing most of the unsown ground was not cultivated so would take less harm; soil with a good tilth can quickly turn to mud when it rains. For these reasons many powered cultivators are now designed to carry a suitable seed drill as well so that the ground is prepared and seeded in one operation.

Rotary cultivators proved ideal for incorporating plant residues back into the soil. It was also found that repeated cultivations of land infested with couch grass could weaken the roots (rhizomes), providing a promising way of controlling both couch grass and bracken.

One of the more surprising uses of powered

Above: Even more substantial is this massive Knight Triple-Press, whose very heavy packing rollers at the back supplement the cultivator legs in front. Again the intention is to achieve as much soil preparation as possible in one pass.

cultivators has been in road building, where contractors use them to loosen the foundations before regrading. On suitable soil the topsoil can be removed and cement spread loose on the surface of the subsoil and mixed in. When this mixture is moistened and mixed again it behaves and sets as concrete.

While not strictly soil-engaging implements, rollers of all descriptions can be a useful aid to producing tilth under the right conditions. The most widely used roller is, of course, the tractor wheel itself. Under certain conditions where there is a modest amount of wheel slip the weight of the wheel plus the slipping action can have a most marked effect in producing a tilth quite independently of the implement that it is pulling.

Flat rollers were well known as horse implements. A later type that became popular was the Cambridge roller, which consists of a large number of individual cast-iron wheels mounted on a common axle, each able to rotate separately. This meant that they very slightly moved in relation to each other, which made it more difficult for soil to build up on the rollers. Their shape, with a prominent ridge in the centre, was very effective in breaking up smaller clods and firming and consolidating the ground.

Drivers usually enjoyed using Cambridge rollers. They were relatively light to pull along on firm soil and had a very broad working width, being often used in gangs, so there was a good output of work to show. Since they were at their best under dry conditions the weather was usually fine when they were in use. One important use was firming down cereal crops in the spring after winter frosts. What better tractor-driving job could there be? With the sun shining, spring in the air, and enough crop growth to prevent kicking up a dust cloud, no wonder the tractor driver would be smiling with pleasure.

A more recent roller development is the Flexi-coil, which is effectively a spiral made from square-section steel. As it rolls it has a scrubbing action, which breaks up clods very effectively.

Much smaller rollers are used behind some forms of power cultivator. These are made up of rods in various sections and have a useful firming and consolidating action with a certain amount of breaking up of crumbs of soil.

Some seed drills now use pneumatic tyres to consolidate the ground behind the drill. They firm in the seed so that the soil is firmly in contact with it. This ensures that it receives the necessary nutrients and moisture as efficiently as possible.

7. Sowing The Seed

Left and below: Larkworthy of Worcester made this horse-drawn four-row root drill, which is typical of the sort of implement that could be built by a workshop equipped to build wagons. The shares, or coulters, are raised and lowered by the crude but effective windlass of chain wrapped around the wooden drum. Metal components are restricted to the levelling mechanism for the seed box, the drive cogs, and a few bolts. Since these would probably have been bought in, drills of this type could be manufactured with only basic woodworking tools, which meant that many local makers could supply their own local markets.

Top right: A buckled leather belt transmits the drive to this root drill. With a choice of pulley sizes the seed rate could be varied relatively easily. The unknown Yorkshire maker still used a wooden superstructure but more ironwork for the wheels, rollers and axle.

Below right: Smyth's of Peasenhall, Suffolk, used metal coulter arms and cast frame brackets, but in many ways the design is traditional. Originally this drill would have been horse-drawn but has been modified with a simple tractor hitch. Smyth had a good reputation as a drill-maker, and its design of coulter was widely copied due to its ability to make a slot for the seed to drop in without becoming blocked. Tactfully, other makers described it as the 'Suffolk pattern'. The wooden handle was cranked to rotate the drum and lift the coulters.

Before a crop can grow, seed has to be sown in the tilth. The earliest way of sowing the seed was by hand broadcasting, whereby the sower walked across the field scattering handfuls of seed over a certain width of ground. Travelling backwards and forwards across the field, a skilled sower could achieve a fairly uniform distribution of seed. When this scattered seed was harrowed in, it would germinate and grow.

However, not only did the seeds grow, but also any weed seeds that were lying dormant in the ground. If recognised, these weeds could be controlled by hand hoeing or even by hand weeding, but until the person hoeing could be certain of distinguishing them from the crop they had to be left to grow.

The early 18th century agriculturist Jethro Tull is generally credited with the idea of a seed drill that would plant seed in straight rows. Anything seen growing that was not in the row could be considered a weed without needing to be identified. His technique was known as 'horse husbandry', his big improvement being the use of a horse hoe between the rows to kill or control most of the weeds. A powered implement was being used to replace a skilled manual job. As well as removing the skill needed to identify a potential weed, this technique increased the area covered by the horse hoeing team. Two other consequences followed that recur time and again. Horse hoeing was physically nearly as hard a job, but more work got done in a day. Yet only part of the job was being done. Hoeing weeds from within the row still needed good men on a hand hoe. Since this type of hoeing required more concentration, Tull's new machine meant fewer people were working just as hard but achieving more.

81

Top left: To farmers used to traditional wooden grain drills the Ferguson drill appeared rather light. When raised, as here, the parallelogram linkage lifted the disc coulters clear of the ground and disengaged the seeders. When lowered, springs helped keep the disc coulters in work. The drill also has a fertiliser box, so that fertiliser could be applied close to the seed to give it a good start. The feed mechanism is so designed that the driver can see that seed is being discharged down all the tubes by looking back from his seat. With no platform to carry a second man, this was clearly intended as a one-man implement.

Below left: The MF 30 combined seed and fertiliser drill was a modern descendant of the early wooden drills. The wheels now carry pneumatic tyres but still drive the seeder mechanism, while the substantial rear footboard has had an extra modified wooden shelf added to facilitate tipping in the bags of seed and fertiliser. A second set of metering devices and tubes feeds fertiliser to each row. In front of the two spectators are spring tines mounted to eradicate the wheel mark left by the drill.

When the idea was first adopted even cereal crops were planted in sufficiently wide rows to permit hoeing between them, which did provide a very effective form of weed control. It also made it possible for an individual to manage a larger area of land and therefore grow more crops for sale.

A seed drill's function is to open up some form of channel in the soil, meter some seed into the open channel, and usually provide some way of filling in the soil behind the seed. This should leave the ground in a condition where the seed can grow with the minimum of adverse factors.

The metering device was needed to ensure that the seeds were planted at the intended rate, and this was usually achieved by having some form of ground-driven wheel driving the metering mechanism; such an arrangement ensured the same application rate regardless of forward speed. Since the seeds were planted at more or less the same rate throughout the field, there would be a more uniform germination than with broadcasting.

Drilling seeds in rows is now widely accepted, although the use of sprays has replaced hoeing in cereal crops allowing narrower spacing.

Even today most seed drills incorporate the features established by Tull. The coulters (the components that open up the channel) are mounted in such a way that each can rise and fall independently of its neighbours to cope with ground conditions. Being pivoted fairly rigidly on a crossbar their side-by-side spacing remains uniform.

The seed is carried in bulk in some sort of container. From there it is metered out and travels by means of a tube to the coulter, where it is able to drop to the ground. Some form of covering device is then usually provided to force soil back over the seed to provide the first protection. Coulters, metering device and seed box are assembled into one implement, which is either mounted on the tractor or supported on its own wheels hitched behind the tractor.

Top left: This cumbersome frame was developed by the NIAE to allow a drill to be towed behind another implement. At the tractor end it pivots above the three-point linkage, allowing the drill to swing clear.

Below left: At the same time the NIAE tried to improve safety for the operator riding on the drill by adding a rear bar and 'mudguards' to protect the wheels. While this was a development project, later in 1974 a similar device was offered commercially.

Above: When time was really pressing this Yates of Malton seed drill came into its own. Coupled to a two-furrow plough, it dropped seed into the newly ploughed furrows. Tilth conditions might not be ideal, but at least the crop was sown. With some form of harrow behind to assist with covering the seed, the whole job was done in one pass. This technique proved useful during World War 2 for drilling into newly reclaimed land.

Below: Direct drilling was carried out into the remains of the previous crop without ploughing. This needed a really robust drill, as the coulters had to be able to cut through uncultivated soil.

A variety of different designs have been applied to meet these objectives. Early drills were fairly crude, being made by local craftsmen, typically the local wagon builder, but eventually some of the more enterprising drill-makers realised that if they could make them in larger numbers they could make them more cheaply. To get more orders they would need to be sold in other areas by dealers, often other local firms who had been previously making drills.

In this way certain companies began to specialise in the manufacture of seed drills. Because they were specialising they could afford to buy in or manufacture more accurate components for seed metering, for example. In turn this improved the performance and accuracy of their drills compared with other locally manufactured examples. Even so, up until World War 2 most drill manufacturers enjoyed a local reputation over a few counties rather than an international one.

With the urgent need for implements during World War 2, many American and Australian seed drills were imported. These were mass-produced and formed a useful source of inspiration for other drill manufacturers. Research had also shown that if fertiliser was applied close to but not actually touching the seed, it gave the maximum benefit to growth. Combined seed drills were therefore developed that applied both seed and fertiliser by different spouts at the same time to each row.

The width of a drill was restricted by the power needed to pull it under difficult ground conditions. With horse teams drills were narrow enough to pass through most gateways, but with tractors more output was needed, and pulling a drill faster was the first obvious answer. However, accuracy suffered and converted horse drills started to fall to bits. Wider drills were then generally seen as the answer, while some users improvised hitches to pull two existing drills behind one tractor.

To prevent overlapping or missing ground, most drills carried some form of marker device that scratched a line in the surface of the field. With this guide for steering it was easier to make sure that the rows matched up. Most horsemen and tractor drivers took a great pride in producing straight rows with no misses or overlaps, and this called for accurate steering, especially with a horse team. When labour was plentiful one man would guide the horses while a second man concentrated on steering the drill by means of a fore-carriage, with a third following the drill to detect any blockages.

With a tractor suffering from wear or slack in the steering system, achieving straight lines became more difficult. It was still the practice for a helper

Top: The two discs running at an angle tended to cut through any surface mat, opening up a channel for the seed to drop into behind.

Above: As the discs had a tendency to ride out of work, direct drills had to be solidly constructed. The substantial springs transferred much of that weight to the coulters.

to ride on the footboard of the drill, his main job being to make sure that all the seed rows were being sown and no blockages were occurring under the drill. He was also very useful in replenishing the seed and later the fertiliser in the drill.

Because of the nature of the seeding mechanism there was usually a delay after moving off before seed reached the soil. If a stop was made in the middle of the field a cluster of seed would fall down the tube and be left at that point, but sowing would not resume until the drill had moved forward a few feet to restart the mechanism. A conscientious helper on the footboard would therefore scatter a double handful of seed over the area where the drill first moved off to compensate for the fact that there had been a stop.

As drills became wider it eventually became necessary to come up with some sort of arrangement so that they could be moved lengthways from field to field. This could be done by fitting transporter wheels to the drill itself, or by using some form of specialised trailer.

While the design of the top end of the drill was changing, attention was also being paid to the coulter mechanism beneath. If it was made more robust, then effectively the drill could carry out a cultivation operation at the same time as applying the seed, which would offer a reduction in the amount of preparation needed in the field. Requiring more effort to pull it, even a narrow drill could then make effective use of tractor power.

These evolved into what were known as direct drills. As they were able to break their way through the uncultivated surface, drilling and cultivation was done in one operation. For a time direct drilling

Above: A Russian technique was to attach the seed drill offset, taking the pull direct from the power unit's rear hub and a steady under the cab steps. This offered two possibilities: the fixing of a matching drill on the other side and one behind, or the attachment of a heavy-duty implement behind to use the full power of the Liaz four-wheel-drive tractor to prepare the ground for drilling. *RLM*

Right: A one-pass outfit built up on a brand-new Renault Ceres for a publicity photograph. In one pass a weathered ploughed field is worked down and sown. While also rather cumbersome-looking at first sight, this outfit is doing a job that would have needed perhaps three or even four tractor and implement combinations. One important advantage is that there is no partly cultivated land to take harm from sudden rain before it has been sown. *RLM*

enjoyed a considerable vogue, and often followed a spray treatment, which controlled any weeds that had germinated. By saving the necessity of ploughing and cultivation, direct drilling reduced the need for tractor and implement power at a time of the year when both were in short supply.

Another line of thought was pneumatic distribution from a central metering point. Instead of having a full-width hopper and all the complications that entailed, the outer parts of the drill consisted simply of coulters fed by tubes from a central pneumatic metering unit. These outer wings could be folded up to reduce the width of the drill when passing through gateways.

Once pneumatic seeding had been demonstrated it was realised that it was quite possible to meter supplies to one or two extra rows at very little additional cost. This became a cost-effective way of building wider drills. Somebody had another thought. With a metering unit able to supply grain at the correct quantity down each tube, why does

Top left: Pneumatic drills, such as this Accord, have central metering. From there the seed is blown down flexible tubes to the individual coulter. By making the coulter support arms tubular the seed can fall down them and straight into the coulters. Behind them is a row of spring tines, which disturb the soil enough to cover the seed. While the seed drill can be used on its own, it can also be combined with a power harrow. In this particular outfit the cultivator is being carried on top of a Lely Roterra. To avoid wheel marks the New Holland 8560 has been fitted with twin rear wheels. Under favourable conditions an outfit like this can travel over ploughed ground to produce a satisfactory tilth and drill the seed all in one pass. One driver is doing the equivalent of four or five jobs with trailed implements. With less chance for the ground to dry out between operations, the seed will be drilled into moister soil, giving it a better start.

there have to be a special drill mechanism beneath? Why not put some relatively simple coulters behind an existing field implement that could produce the tilth into which the seed could be sown all in one pass. This led to a trend of mounting a seed drilling mechanism on top of a powered cultivator, the aim being to reduce the number of cultivation operations needed before the seed could be drilled. As with any other form of rotary cultivation the ground remained virtually undisturbed until seeding was ready to take place, and in the event of unexpected rain the minimum amount of soil was affected before the seed was drilled.

Today the practice is often to plough the land, possibly with a furrow press attached, then leave it undisturbed until drilling time. One pass with a combined tiller and seed drill outfit will get the seed into the soil and leave it firmly covered and ready to grow.

Developments like this make effective use of today's powerful four-wheel-drive tractors, and explain why it is becoming less common to see a tractor and implement actually at work in an arable field. These modern outfits can cope with much larger areas of ground, making it practical for a farmer to sow his neighbour's ground. Indeed, the same outfit may be shared between several farms, such an arrangement reducing the amount of machinery actually to be seen in the field.

Grain drills used to be calibrated in terms of the weight of seed applied per acre, or indeed even the volume of seed expressed as bushels per acre. Each grain that germinates will grow into a plant, and during the last 20 years it has been recognised that the most important factor is the number of grains applied per acre or hectare. For this reason grain is often sold with a declared weight per thousand

Above: Tramlines at an unusually close spacing are clearly visible in the newly emerged cereal crop. The darker lines are where the drill has slightly overlapped to form two closely spaced rows.

Left: By the time the crop is harvested the tramlines are much more compacted than the rest of the field. Special attention from a two-leg ripper restores the soil condition before the whole field is cultivated ready for the next crop.

grains. With this information the application rate can be worked out in weight to give the correct number of grains per hectare applied. This is a finely balanced decision. Too much grain increases the cost of seed per acre, while too little can reduce the eventual yield. The aim is to sow as little grain as possible without affecting yield. It does of course mean trying to predict what weather conditions will be like after the grain has been sown.

Having spent so long trying to build seed drills that can sow every row accurately and at the correct spacing, drill manufacturers were somewhat disconcerted 20-odd years ago when customers started to ask them for the facility to leave an occasional row blank. Known as the tramline system, the blank rows served as a steering guide for tractors travelling through the crop when spraying or fertilising. The idea was that if the drill spacing was done correctly the tramlines or rows with no growth would be left at exactly the correct spacing so that there would be no overlapping of the sprayer. The fertiliser spreader could also be calibrated so that even with overlaps the final result was a uniform application of top dressings.

While tramlines do represent a reduction in crop yield, this is offset by the improvements following more accurate timing of spray and fertiliser applications. Indeed, just like Jethro Tull's original rows, tramlines still serve as a guide to farmers wishing to control weeds.

Above right: Sugar beet seed in its natural form can produce several plants, but with careful preparation individual seeds can be produced that only germinate into a single plant. When sown at regular spacing, such seed avoids the need to remove surplus plants by hoeing or singling. The seed goes in the individual boxes with fertiliser placed separately by each row. Even spacing eliminates overcrowding and gives each beet a chance to grow to a size that will yield the greatest amount of sugar from a given area.

Precision seeders can plant such seed evenly and correctly spaced, but very accurate driving is needed as any kinks will affect future cultivations and harvesting. This Massey Ferguson 590 has the seeders mounted behind, which means that even a small steering correction will increase the swing. For best results a fine tilth and slow travel speed are needed. The required concentration is very tiring, so the driver is probably not too sorry to have been rained off temporarily.

The spread of tramlines has coincided with manufacturers changing from imperial to metric widths for their drills. Complications followed as farmers wrestled with the various permutations of drill, sprayer and fertiliser spreader needed to adopt tramlining. At first all sorts of curious combinations were adopted to try and get the tramlines at the correct spacing. Most times a row needed to be drilled, so how did you memorise that perhaps every sixth turn with the drill you had to block off two rows to leave the tramline? Any lapse of memory would mean that the two rows were in the wrong drilling and the spacing was incorrect. One portion of the field would either be getting double treatment or none at all. All sorts of mechanical devices were proposed, but eventually most of them worked on the basis that every time the drill was lowered for the fifth or sixth time the tramlining mechanism would come into operation automatically and block off a couple of rows.

If the tramlines were laid out correctly in the field they did a considerable amount to reduce damage to the crop when fertiliser or sprays were being applied at later stages of growth, especially when late applications were made to provide a final spurt for the growing crop to increase the yields. Steering the sprayer also became much less tricky; all that was needed was simply to follow the tracks, which was much easier than trying to judge distances at the end of a very long sprayer boom.

The further apart the tramlines are spaced, the less growing space is lost. Adopting tramlines has encouraged the use of sprayers and fertiliser spreaders with the ability to cover wider strips in one pass. One snag is that wider machines are more inconvenienced by isolated trees, electricity poles and other obstructions in an otherwise open field.

Other forms of specialised drill are used for particular crops; potatoes, for example, are planted as tubers rather than individual seeds. In the same way sugar beet has very specialised requirements for drilling its seed. The seed as harvested is in the form of clusters, but planting a cluster results in several plants geminating in one spot. For the beet to grow to full size, the plants need to be carefully hoed, ensuring that the surviving plant grows vigorously. Singling beet by hand hoe was a tedious back-breaking job involving the destruction of many viable plants. Today sugar beet seed is rubbed or milled then pelleted, so that each pellet will produce only a single viable plant. Precision seeders can then place prepared individual seeds at intervals.

Left: When conditions are right it is vital to push on. As dusk falls, this six-row Accord is drilling beet into rich dark soil in Lincolnshire. Early drilling helps to ensure maximum growth and the highest yield of sugar.

Below: A contrast in equipment: the Ferguson and plough, and the seed drill partly visible on the extreme left, were designed in the 1940s. One driver did one job with perhaps 24hp available. The Fastrac behind has six or seven times the power, and its implement can cultivate the ground, sow the seed, and firm the seedbed. While the Ferguson driver filled his own seed drill, a modern drill needs a handler to transport big bags of seed to fill it. However, the modern equipment needs much less effort and is much quicker in use. The main problem is that such high-output equipment requires considerably more land to be cultivated each year before it becomes economic to use.

8. Hoeing, Spraying and Fertilising

Weeds are defined as any plants growing where they are not wanted. Left uncontrolled they compete with the growing crop for nutrients, light and moisture, resulting in lower yields, usually greater difficulty in harvesting, and possible contamination of the harvested crop.

Most workmen who used a hand hoe seriously had a dream that one day a machine would pass over the field and kill off the weeds without this laborious and back-breaking work. For centuries this remained a forlorn hope, and weed control was restricted to hoeing and cultivation, but in time various implements did the majority of the hoeing between the rows, leaving the more intricate work for the hoemen.

An early sprayed weedkiller was sulphuric acid, which, if sprayed on a suitable crop at the right time, would attack certain forms of weed, while the spray would run off the leaves of the crop being treated with the minimum of damage. Sulphuric acid enjoyed another use as a means of killing off potato haulm, preventing blight being transmitted from the leaves back down to the tubers.

Other early users of sprays were fruit-growers, who used to apply limewash in the winter to kill or control mites and pests that, left unchecked, would damage the blossoms and fruits when they were being formed.

The first really significant step in weed control was the development of so-called hormone weedkillers, which were intended to stimulate certain types of plant to excessive growth. The affected weeds grew to excess and actually harmed themselves. After a week or two, to his surprise, the farmer would see that virtually all the treated weeds were actually twisted and dying off while the crop continued to grow unaffected. For the farmer and our dreamer on his hoe, this represented nothing short of a miracle.

How were these wonder chemicals to be applied? Maybe a pint or half a pint of the product needed to be mixed with, perhaps, 40 gallons of water,

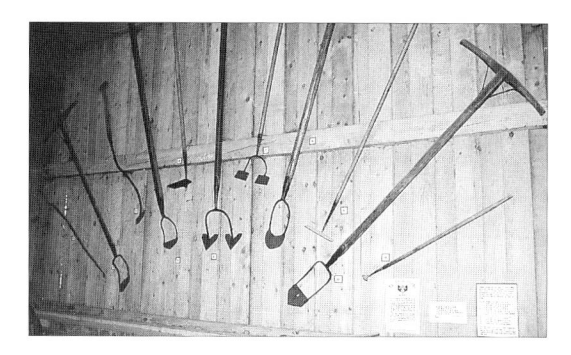

Above: A selection of hoes displayed at the Yorkshire Farming Museum. Most people who have used one commercially would reckon that this is the best place for a hand hoe!

Below: Even the small tank capacity of this early Ferguson crop-sprayer was sufficient for perhaps several acres depending on the application rate. The booms were of simple construction and folded by hand, while the pump was driven from the PTO.

Above: This sprayer is mounted on a Ford Ferguson that had been used for many years as a specialist spraying tractor. In this role it was equipped with narrow, large-diameter row-crop wheels. Allman of Chichester, Sussex, made both the sprayer and the wheels.

Left: Ransomes offered the Cropguard, which is shown here fitted on a Ferguson that has been modified to give extra clearance. One limit on the size of the tank offered was the lifting and carrying capacity of the tractor with which it would be used.

which would be enough to treat about an acre of crops. Metric equivalents today would be about 1 litre in 400 litres to treat a hectare.

Early sprayers were relatively simple, consisting of a tank, pump and boom. The solution was pumped to the fixed-interval spray nozzles on the boom, a valve restricting the flow to a particular pressure. Any surplus was pumped back into the tank to keep the contents agitated and mixed. Varying the speed of travel, the pressure or the type of nozzles fitted could alter the application rate.

One early sprayer was even more basic. A simple air compressor was used to pressurise a 40-gallon barrel, and the pressurised solution was fed through a controller to the spray boom. Within a few years nearly every farm had acquired its own sprayer and

Top right: **Rural branches of Boots the Chemist used to sell large quantities of weed- and pest-control chemicals. This mounted crop-duster, manufactured for Boots by Horstine Farmery, which specialised in crop-dusting systems, was used to apply these specialist powders. Needing no water, crop-dusters could cover larger areas for one filling. The 'body' on the right is the remains of a scarecrow, a more traditional pest-control system!**

Centre right: **If a tractor could carry a slightly bigger tank it could cover a larger area between fills. A moulded plastic tank could be shaped to fit more snugly to the back of a tractor, bringing the centre of gravity closer to the rear axle. RLM**

Bottom right: **Mounting the spray tank on wheels was another way of increasing the area that could be sprayed between refills.**

Above: A reminder that constant attention is needed to keep on top of weeds! Once parked out of use, it has not taken long for weeds to grow up around this Chafer sprayer. Such sprayers were often hired by the season, then returned to Chafer each year for overhaul and any improvements for next season. The older iron-wheeled water cart would have been used to move water to livestock, a steam engine, or even to the farmhouse.

Below: As tractors got bigger, mounted sprayers also grew in size. Cleanacres of Andoversford used large-diameter aluminium pipe with support struts to take some of the weight of the actual spray boom.

Above: **British sprayer manufacturers began to face competition from European manufacturers willing to build sprayers with even greater carrying capacities and wider booms. Everard of France built this trailed sprayer.**

had eradicated a tremendous number of weeds.

A few makers followed an alternative route and formulated chemicals as powders. These were less bulky than a diluted chemical, but many sprays were offered only as liquids, which favoured sprayers.

As ever, Nature responded to this new development. Weeds that had been ignored or overshadowed by other more successful competitors flourished in their absence, the spraying actually improving their growing conditions. After a few years farms began to find that species that had previously not been a problem were now troublesome. Scientists responded to these challenges by developing other more sophisticated sprays to control these new problem weeds as they emerged.

Other scientists were developing sprays that tackled the mildews and fungi that could affect the final yield of cereal crops. More sophisticated equipment was needed to apply these sprays, but it was often cost-effective to spray the crop much later, especially for some of the specialised fungal treatments.

Meanwhile plant breeders were developing new varieties that were more responsive to these new forms of management. It started to make good economic sense to spray each crop several times a year, so a much more sophisticated sprayer could be justified on the farm. It was also sensible to use as wide a sprayer as possible to reduce the amount of damage caused when driving through a growing crop, which enabled crops to be sprayed at a later stage of growth, and ensured that a bigger area was covered in a given time. As farms got bigger, sprayers were working harder. The best way of increasing the amount of work a sprayer could do in a day was to fit a larger tank, reducing the number of journeys to refill it. Better formulations allowed lower application rates, again meaning that each tankful covered a bigger area.

A problem with wide sprayers was avoiding overlaps that meant wasteful use of the chemical, while a missed area meant triumphant weeds rearing their heads to the embarrassment of the sprayer operator. As we saw in the previous chapter, the answer proved deceptively simple. Blocking one or two spouts in a seed drill left easily followed tramlines in the growing crop. Match the boom width of the sprayer to these gaps and the driver could achieve a perfect match avoiding over- or under-spraying.

From the beginning a few specialist sprayer

Above: An early 'self-propelled' sprayer, modified from a tractor with the driver's seat moved forward and protected by a cab and filtered air supply. At first sprayers like this were usually built to the specific requirements of one particular farmer. You might think double wheels on the front and triples on the rear look unnecessary, but the winch tractor alongside is a good clue that the ground can get pretty soft.

Left: This self-propelled sprayer was built by Dorman of Cambridge. The tractor was a Ford modified by County to its High Clear specification. The driver enjoyed an air-conditioned cab to keep out the spray, while the two tanks were hinged to permit access to the engine for maintenance. *RLM*

Bottom left: This Iseki 6500 was displayed at the Royal Show one year to gauge reaction. As a 72hp four-wheel-drive tractor it could mount narrow row-crop tyres for work in growing crops, or extra-wide low-pressure tyres for work over soft or wet ground to reduce rutting. Sprayer ruts tend to dry out and harden later in the year, making travel more difficult during harvest. *RLM*

Left: Recognising a demand for self-propelled sprayers, engineers started to build them from first principles. They could be made lighter by building a special chassis and using a smaller engine. This Atkinson of the early 1980s had four-wheel drive and was mounted on flotation tyres to reduce ground pressure.

Below left: Another way of reducing ground pressure was to mount a conventional small tractor sprayer on a commercially available load carrier.

contractors had modified their farm tractors. Extra tanks were mounted around the tractor to increase the carrying capacity, and in farm workshops more drastic modifications increased the potential carrying capacity. Early efforts also included moving the driving position of the tractor in front of the radiator, which left room at the back end to mount a larger spray tank. The opportunity was also taken to improve the ground clearance under the tractor, which reduced the amount of damage caused when passing over a crop.

Other farmers built sprayers on the Mercedes-Benz Unimog chassis. This substantial four-wheel-drive industrial machine could carry a large sprayer mounted in the load-carrying area. From these beginnings a number of specialised firms emerged building self-propelled sprayers. These were rarely existing manufacturers adding to their range, but were usually new and innovative firms building a machine of great complexity from first principles.

Soon, instead of using conventional tractors as the basis of a sprayer, they could unite an engine and transmission to an axle layout of their own choice. Some used hydrostatic transmissions, which allowed all the wheels to be driven hydraulically despite a high frame clearance for passing through crops.

Sprayer designers have a number of problems to cope with. Ideally the forward speed of the sprayer should remain the same whether climbing a hill or descending a slope. For greater accuracy the forward speed is often measured using radar directed at the ground, which eliminates possible error from wheel slip. Maintaining a fixed forward speed calls for plenty of engine power. Many

Above and left: Knight is now recognised as a specialist builder of sprayers, and had the classic beginning. A local customer had a firm idea of the sort of sprayer he needed, so he approached Ron Knight, who had a reputation for building one-off machines. The resulting machine suited so well that other neighbours ordered similar ones. The final results are specialist bits of equipment exactly matched to those customers' requirements, and probably also include plenty of input from the actual operator. Small companies like this can be far more responsive to individual customers, allowing the sort of tailoring that is very different from the way larger companies have to operate. This self-propelled sprayer is mounted on a specialist transport chassis manufactured by Multidrive.

sprayers are mounted on a variety of wheels during the year, and since these will have different rolling radii, the speed for a given transmission setting will be affected.

The operator has plenty to do in controlling the sprayer. With booms extended the job is rather like taxying a medium-sized aircraft. When steering, the driver always has to be aware of the position of the sprayer booms. He may have to fold part of a boom to get past an obstruction such as a mid-field telegraph pole or electricity pylon. The boom also has to be kept away from boundary hedges, while there may be conservation areas, ditches or streams that must not be sprayed.

While watching all this, the operator also has to monitor the pressure of the spray from the pump and the flow rate, and to check that no jets are blocked and that there is sufficient spray in the tank to complete the job. Overall the operator has to ensure that spray is being applied at the correct rate.

Technical knowledge of the sprays being applied is also needed, as well as accuracy in working out application rates and concern for public safety. The weather can affect spraying: too much wind might result in spray drifting from the desired target, while rain will have the effect of diluting the spray and wasting it. Sprayer operators now have to hold

Right: When spraying in standing crops the lowest point on a tractor is usually the axle. Instead of fitting ever bigger wheels, sprayer designers might opt for hydrostatic drive, which also allows all-wheel steering, more clearance and infinitely variable forward speeds. While this arrangement is probably more expensive to build, a knowledgeable customer will appreciate the benefits and be quite willing to accept the extra cost.

Centre right: Another specialist manufacturer is Bateman of Devon, whose sophisticated 2001 was introduced 10 years ahead of its date. At that time its specification was far in advance of anything available from the major multinational manufacturers. Four-wheel steering meant only one set of wheel tracks when turning, the cab offered the operator good visibility, and there was enough clearance to fit bigger wheels when the crop had grown. *RLM*

Bottom right: For the customer willing to wait a few years the larger manufacturers would eventually catch up. Fitting larger and narrower wheels to a JCB Fastrac gave this customer the clearance he needed. With so many Fastracs in use, makers can offer in quantity a standardised sprayer to fit. Adding the two together produces a serviceable self-propelled spraying outfit that can revert to a normal tractor and a parked sprayer. Such an outfit, with a good turn of speed on the road, can spray individual fields with the minimum of wasted time, even if they are widely scattered.

Left: British manufacturer Gem specialised from the beginning in wide sprayers. For larger farms with more spray applications it made sense to purchase a specialist self-propelled machine, as the example built by Gem shown here.

Centre left: As demonstrated here, most spray booms can swing in relation to the sprayer. Depending on the type of boom specified, this can either be adjusted by the driver, or the weight of the boom itself tends to bring it back to the horizontal. The vertical mast at the rear guides the boom as it is raised or lowered.

Below: Even mounted sprayers now have wide booms to reduce the amount of travelling and crop damage while spraying a given area. This Allman 1,000-litre machine was being demonstrated in 2000. The white container is for clean water for the driver to wash with. Modern tractor cabs make spraying a more pleasant job.

Top right: As with its self-propelled sprayers, Knight's trailed sprayers, made in a purpose-built factory in Rutland, are still specified and built in close co-operation with the eventual user, which can show itself in the type of boom chosen. Here, folding and unfolding the boom is entirely controlled from the tractor cab.

Right: This is an early horse-drawn fertiliser spreader modified for tractor use. It was built by Ogle, which is still in business in Ripley, Derbyshire. The fertiliser was metered out through the partly covered holes on to the board where it ran down to the ground.

a certificate of competence and demonstrate that they have the technical knowledge to spray safely and to minimise the potential risk to neighbouring crops, residents or pedestrians. Extensive records have to be kept of spray treatments and the conditions at the time the treatment was applied. As a result, spray applications are more accurately matched to the needs of a particular crop.

Today many of these sprayers will be covering considerable areas each year. This means that customers are willing to invest large sums in ensuring that the sprayer is fully equipped to make the operator's job as simple as possible.

Farmers have long known that manure is good for crops, but not every farm has sufficient available, so it has to be supplemented with bought-in fertility. At first this came from accumulated bird droppings known as guano, by-products of the woollen industry known as shoddy, and manure from town stables. Often near towns there were exceedingly fertile farms known as sewage farms, where processed sewage was pumped on the land in large quantities; while these produce a response, supplies are limited and transport expensive. The answer is to obtain extra nutrients from chemical fertilisers, otherwise known as artificial manures.

These have three main elements:

- Nitrogen was originally sourced as a by-product of making town gas, and was often sold as sulphate of ammonia. Later research came up with an industrial process that allowed nitrogen to be extracted from the air or petroleum by-products like natural gas. Four-fifths of the atmosphere we breathe is nitrogen, yet most plants still need help to make the best use of it.

Left: A close-up of the metering mechanism of an early tractor fertiliser spreader. The disc rotates slowly, carrying fertiliser that is knocked off by the tines on the rotating shaft.

Below left: The same system is used on this tractor-drawn spreader. The working width of 8ft was the maximum possible if the spreader was to pass through a normal farm gateway.

- Potassium is derived mainly from weathered rock. Large deposits occur where seas have long since dried up. A large deposit is being mined in Cleveland in the UK.

- Phosphorus also occurs naturally. Some rock formations containing particularly large concentrations are mined and ground up.

Acid soil cannot make the best use of nutrients, but lime neutralises acidity in the soil to help plant growth. Lime is mined from natural rock formations in various parts of the country.

At first these elements were bought as individual items to spread on the land, but today most fertilisers are sold as blends or compounds. Packing has varied from hessian, paper and plastic sacks to big bags weighing a tonne or half a tonne. Moisture makes fertilisers cake and become difficult to spread, so modern fertilisers are normally produced as granules or prills (pellets). Most are compounds with a mixture of ingredients. To get the best from them they are either placed close to the plant seed or tuber, or uniformly distributed over the whole field. Early machines had a number of metering mechanisms to drop the fertiliser in rows. From this was developed the combined seed and fertiliser drill mentioned in the previous chapter, able to place the fertiliser close to the seed. Another alternative was to drive a spinning disc and trickle fertiliser on to it, the fertiliser being thrown off the disc at high speed.

Initially the results were rough and ready, but as the characteristics of the fertiliser granules were more tightly controlled and predictable, results improved. Now spinning disc spreaders can hurl granules or prills considerable distances, giving greater working widths.

Trials and research have shown that little and often gives the best results with most crops. If

Top right and Centre right: Trevor K. Knox was one of the Ferguson design team before starting a specialist machinery import company. One of his suppliers, New Idea, came up with an answer to narrow gateways and wide fertiliser spreaders. Once in the field the two halves of the spreader could be unfolded and locked to make a much wider machine.

Bottom: British manufacturer Gem specialised from the beginning in wide sprayers; this example is spraying recently emerged potatoes in Hereforshire. The white blob on the back is a small electrically driven spinner for scattering slug pellets if required.

Top left: The most effective way of reducing ruts is to keep the wheels off the ground! Aerial crop-spraying can be cost-effective for a large area. The pilot of this Piper Pawnee is certainly getting close to his work, but while crop-spraying can be spectacular to watch, it calls for intense concentration from the pilot. The high risk and the need for a payload mean that these are solo flights.

Left: The sprayer boom is mounted just behind the wings.

Below left: For locust and mosquito spraying, fogging nozzles mean that much larger areas can be covered in a single flight. Aerial spraying has always been a job for a specialist contractor.

Below right: Modern spinning-disc spreaders work on the same principle, but more sophisticated design and more uniform granules mean that they can cover a much greater width. At the Royal Show 2000 a competitor is demonstrating the correct operation of the spreader to a judge in the 'Tractor Driver of the Year' competition. Entering such competitions is a good incentive for operators to get the best from their machinery.

fertiliser is applied in the autumn, newly planted seed can only make effective use of a small amount of the nutrients. Some may be washed out of the soil over the winter and wasted. A good time for the next application is when growth resumes in the spring, with perhaps a subsequent top dressing of mainly nitrogen-rich fertiliser to encourage the growth of plenty of leaf. It is these leaves that benefit from the sunshine to produce the crop that will eventually be harvested.

As tramline spacings became wider other methods such as pneumatic discharge were used to improve accuracy of applications. As with sprays, farmers have to perform a balancing act. Up to a point the more fertiliser that is applied, the more crop will be harvested, which in turn means more food for us to eat. While applying no fertiliser would save money, the yield would be far lower. Variations in the price of fertiliser and the crop being grown will also alter the balance. Other complications are the potential of the soil in which the crop is being grown, and the needs of the buyer.

To help with the question of how much fertiliser to apply, sophisticated computer programs have been developed to act on the farmer's intentions and convert them into application instructions. Some spreaders can interact with yield maps from combines to vary the application rate in different parts of the field in response to the previous year's recorded yields.

As an alternative to mounted or trailed fertiliser spreaders, some users mount them as alternative bodies for self-propelled sprayers. This gets more work out of the chassis and can make use of the same monitoring equipment.

Much is said about organic farming, where crop residues and manure are returned to the soil. However efficient an organic grower is, some of the nutrients are removed from the farm each year in the form of crops harvested and sold, and this has to be replaced from somewhere or yields are likely to decline in the long run.

Right: The spinning disc on this Lister trailed spreader is driven by the axle of the transport wheels. Depending on the speed of travel, fertiliser can be spread over a useful width.

Below right: Cereal crops respond well to an application of fertiliser early in the spring, but a heavy tractor will leave ruts if the soil is wet. In 1981 this six-wheeled lightweight load carrier was fitted with a Vicon Varispreader with a separate engine to drive it. Instead of a spinning disc, this design of spreader relies on a wagging spout to distribute the fertiliser.

Right: A fertiliser spreader is usually adjusted so that if the tractor is operated as intended the whole field will have fertiliser applied at the intended rate. This experimental rig takes a different approach. This front-mounted apparatus observes the condition of the crop and assesses its need for nitrogen; this assessment is used to constantly adjust the calibration of the mounted Amazone spreader. A similar effect could be obtained by driver observation and choice of gears. Changing down a gear on the tractor increases the application rate, while changing up a gear decreases it. *RLM*

9. Transport and Mechanical Handling

Much of the work on a farm has always involved transporting material from place to place - dung, fertiliser, seeds, produce, grain, fodder, water and winter-feed. Traditionally this has required manual effort to get the material loaded, a means of transport, and further manual effort to unload, spread or stack it.

Wheeled Transport

Transport in horse days was by four-wheeled wagon, two-wheeled cart with fixed sides, or a two-wheeled flat cart. Where there were steep slopes on the farm a sledge might be used to transport produce downhill to the farm buildings. Any of these vehicles could be built by a local wagon-maker, wheelwright or carpenter. The exact description of a particular builder would vary according to what formed the main part of his business - many of them had a useful sideline acting as the local undertaker! Locally grown timber was the main material needed for construction. Any necessary metalwork could be made by a local

Top left: As well as horses, oxen were occasionally used for haulage. Each year one young animal would be added to the team to replace the oldest member, which would be butchered for its tough but flavoursome meat. But even by the end of the 19th century, when this photograph was taken in Sussex, they were regarded as old-fashioned.

Centre left: The two-wheeled cart was the main transport method on most farms. To increase its carrying capacity for loose hay, extension ladders have been fitted front and rear. A good horseman planned his load so that it was balanced over the wheels and imposed the minimum load on the horse.

Bottom left: When this tip-cart was built in the 1930s the builder fitted a brand-new axle and wheel set, which was available as a complete unit. Besides saving the job of making traditional wheels, the tyres and better bearings made the cart much lighter to pull. This cart was being offered for sale 60 years later after being pulled out of storage with its offside shaft broken off.

Top right: This is another 1930s cart with pneumatic tyres, and is arranged to tip. By releasing the pin the body and load are so nearly balanced that one man should be able to tip the body with one strong heave; but with no arrangement to restrict the amount of tip, it was all or nothing. The body is made out of individual pieces of timber, probably elm, cut to size. Note how a wooden drawbar has been made to convert the trailer for tractor use.

Above right: For this early farm trailer the body is mounted higher and extends over the wheels. The sides can be folded down and are fitted with detachable extension sides. The rear tailboard can also be folded down and extensions are provided to protect the tailboard from damage if the trailer is backed into a wall. All the ironwork has been bought in from a specialist bodybuilder supplier, while the sides and tailboard are made from standard-width pieces of planking. Despite its traditional appearance, the builder has clearly started to study modern methods of construction. Its only disadvantage is that it is rather high to load, although for most jobs it would be possible to put on most of the load with a side down before putting it up to finish the job.

Below right: Early tractor-trailers were converted wagons built in the traditional manner, as the lower example seen here, and the drawbar or shafts were attached at the front of the turntable. From the 1930s some trailer builders started to use axles from scrapped lorries, as seen in the upper trailer, the rear axle of which is mounted on two substantial wooden blocks held in place by steel brackets folded out of flat steel. The only other iron items are the flat steel corner-pieces and the rear towing arrangement of a hook and a simple drawbar, which could be used to pull either a second trailer or a hay-loader. Such trailers were quicker and cheaper to make than the pattern underneath, and since it was probably built before 1947 there was no legal requirement for working brakes. The substantial trellises alongside the trailers are detachable hay ladders fitted front and rear to hold a bigger load of hay or sheaves.

Bottom right: This trailer has been modified during its life with a lorry rear axle replacing the original. To take advantage of its extra carrying capacity, a larger body has been added to what started life as a Ferguson trailer. (Note that it is advertising a Farmers' Market, a venture that provides a chance for farmers to trade directly with the public.)

Left: This trailer had been retired from British Road Services, and a dolly with a drawbar and a lorry-type coupling added. With one or more dollies several old trailers can be used to provide both haulage and temporary storage for loads. Big four-wheel articulated trailers like this are useful for moving bales and loads like seed and fertiliser at planting time. As these jobs normally arise when ground conditions are good, heavy loads can be moved.

Below left: A long four-wheeler also lends itself to mechanical loading and unloading, and with a flat-eight bale grab, a handler can load or unload eight bales at a time. These packs can be built into loads and stacks, but they are not bonded as they would be if the bales were stacked individually. However, the time and effort saved mean that this disadvantage is acceptable.

blacksmith or later obtained from more specialised suppliers.

Probably the first mechanical aid for transport on the farm was the tipping horse-cart. This reduced the need to shovel or fork off the load; instead it was possible to release a catch and upend the body of the cart. In one rush most of the load was discharged. By pegging the tipping mechanism in some way, unloading could be controlled by the horseman with a hand tool; for example, when applying dung to the field, individual heaps could be raked off the cart and left to be spread across the field.

Most horse-and-cart work involved loading and unloading by hand, and much the same applied with the traditional horse-drawn wagon. Some mechanical assistance was, however, available in the 1920s and 1930s. A mechanical hay-loader could be towed behind a wagon, raking up hay off the ground, forcing it up an inclined plane, and allowing it to fall into the wagon (as illustrated in Chapter 3). One or two chaps, whose job was to get it stacked on the wagon, sweated furiously trying to cope with the relentless flow of hay. Considerable effort was needed to pull the loaded wagon plus the hay-loader, and for the horses this was hard and tiring work. The arrival of tractors did little to change the situation. A tractor was better placed to pull the wagon and hay-loader combination, but the stackers on the wagon probably found the work even harder!

By the time the tractor was introduced the wagons might be 10 to 50 years old, but with some crude modification to the shafts they became the first four-wheel trailers on most farms. Tractors were more powerful than a team of horses, and their solid construction and cleated wheels meant that more shocks were being transmitted to the wagon. As a result the wagons suffered far worse treatment than their builders had anticipated.

The first purpose-built tractor trailers were based very closely on horse-drawn vehicle principles, but

Right: Harry Ferguson's design team took a different approach to trailer design. A substantial fabricated steel chassis and drawbar was the foundation, and the roller-bearing axle was set at the extreme rear, imposing plenty of weight on the tractor. No jack was needed as the pick-up hook on the tractor could raise or lower the drawbar. The sides dropped into pockets in the platform, and their supports were boxed so that they in turn could take extensions. The tailboard could drop right down. With a hydraulic tipping ram underneath the body, it could be tipped to the desired angle from the tractor seat. When they first appeared, the axle layout meant that some local councils tried to class a Ferguson and trailer as an articulated lorry.

to take advantage of the extra power available they offered a greater carrying capacity. Mechanical tipping trailers came into use soon after World War 2, most initially fitted with screw-operated tipping gear. This represented harder work to tip than the balanced arrangement on a cart, but it was rather more controllable.

Methods of construction gradually evolved. Wagons became simpler in construction and were rationalised. Builders started to buy in components like axles and hubs. Tyre-makers started to offer to builders complete assemblies of tyres, axles and wheels. It was soon found that pneumatic tyres and axles from scrapped lorries could be used in place of the old-fashioned wooden wheels. Often these changes were taking place locally at different stages.

This was particularly noticeable in the late 1940s. Peace and better prices meant that trailers of any type were in strong demand. For example, before World War 2 G. C. Smith had been a high-quality coachbuilder in Leicestershire. With few new chassis available on which to build lorry bodies, the company turned to making trailers. However, the craftsmen would not contemplate rough and ready

Above right: After 50 years of use this Ferguson trailer still looks serviceable, if battered. In the background is a Weeks tandem-axle grain trailer with a bigger carrying capacity. The body is made from folded sheet steel, including extension sides to carry grain in bulk.

Right: Taking a closer look at the pressed steel sides, it can be seen how they are built up; the bottom-hinged sides are held in place and an extra panel fitted on top. With a third panel fitted, the body would have sufficient capacity for silage making, while with only a single panel all round the trailer could cope with roots or dung as a load. This style of bodywork is quite satisfactory unless the panels are damaged while removed from the trailer.

Bottom right: The pick-up ring of the Ferguson trailer drawbar is now almost universal, and the shape of this one is a small reminder of a frightening incident! The twist is a sign that at some time the trailer has been tipped over. This often happened while tipping and could be very disconcerting for the tractor driver.

Top left: While Ferguson could justify a carefully designed and profiled drawbar, other makers fabricated them by cutting and welding standard steel profiles. It would be difficult to make the damaged sideboard seen here grain-tight, but by dropping a grain tank inside the existing body the trailer can carry a much bigger load without risk of leakage. Most makers soon adopted Ferguson's set-back axle position to impose more weight on the tractor.

Below left: This Tye trailer from Yorkshire was 27 years old when photographed. Quality timber - Malayan hardwood that withstands weathering - means that it is still serviceable.

work, so trailers were turned out varnished in immaculate style. As lorry chassis became available they returned to that work, and still specialise in horseboxes and mobile libraries to a very high standard of finish.

By contrast, Lamport of Catsgore, Somerset, was a traditional local wagon-builder, but advanced to using a steel drawbar and new axles while retaining a wooden chassis. A screw tipper could be supplied to order. The trailers were immaculately turned out, painted and lined. Even today the firm's workmanship can be admired on trailers still in use. Unfortunately, the firm quietly faded away, unable to compete with the arrival of mass-produced trailers.

Robert Keen at North Stoke near Wallingford wanted trailers to carry more sheaves. By buying complete rolling lorry chassis as scrap he could crudely modify the front axle to be steered by a drawbar. When turning tight corners the tractor might need to drag the front round tighter than it really wanted to, but it did the job. With a flat body and ladders, his trailers were seen as outsized, but they could cope with three times the number of sheaves that a traditional wagon could carry. When he started selling trailers they were always noted for being able to carry big payloads. The company never moved into anything very sophisticated in trailer design, most being flat with no tipping mechanism. Wood was supplied either untreated or sprayed with creosote. With his use of large quantities of local timber, Keen went on to make the widely used North Stoke bale sledge.

Markham Traction offered a trailer that tipped from a pivot near its mid-point. The tipping was done with a hydraulic ram fed either by a hand pump or, if it was pulled by a modern tractor, from the tractor's hydraulic system. Markham later

Above left and left: Wards of Yorkshire favoured a steel frame with timber planking and the choice of a new or, as here, second-hand axle. The steel floor is a later repair, but good workmanship and high-quality hardwood mean that the trailer is still in regular use.

Top right: This hard-used Weeks trailer has a floor badly worn by abuse and overloading. The rear extension shows the difference between an accountant's approach and a farmer's - to carry more bales the substantial extension uses ex-Army pierced tracking and discarded steel angle-iron. In contrast the trailer floor was built with the lightest steel that would do the job.

Centre right: Another way of increasing trailer capacity was by adding an extra timber surround. Even if no more load is carried, it tends to reduce the risk of losing grain over the sides when crossing bumps.

Bottom right: Brakes were required on trailers built after 1947, and the wheel and screw-shaft seen here were used to apply or release the brakes, which might explain the use of a new axle by the maker, Robert Keen. By making the track wider a bigger body could be fitted between the wheels, and with the axle set back this was clearly built for use behind a tractor. Even with the tailboard in place you can see how low the loading height is. With the tailboard removed it would be relatively easy to load sacks of grain in the field. With the extension lips and the front hay ladder, it would also be well suited to carry loose hay or sheaves. Notice the substantial jack to assist with uncoupling and coupling when loaded. About 40 years ago this trailer was loaded with firewood and backed into a shed. In 2000 it was finally unloaded before being offered for sale at Old Sodbury's Vintage Sortout at Newbury!

merged with Martins Cultivators to become Martin Markham, which traded successfully for some years.

Harry Ferguson felt that a trailer should be part of the Ferguson System. He placed the axle at the extreme rear, which imposed plenty of weight on the tractor's rear wheels. Unusually, his design team had a false start with the original hitch, which involved a complex linkage. It was soon replaced by a single drawbar and drop-forged ring, with a matching pick-up hook arrangement fitted to the tractor; the trailer could be coupled from the driver's seat with little exertion. Today the pick-up hitch and ring drawbar is almost universally used. Most Ferguson trailers were supplied as tippers with a hydraulic ram beneath the body.

Joseph Cyril Bamford bought himself a welder and started welding together trailers. With no tradition of working in timber, it made sense to him to build in steel using second-hand materials. From this basis he was soon producing trailers with hydraulic tipping. Instead of concentrating on trailers, he then looked at other implements that could be made using the same processes. His JCB company went on to specialise in the manufacture of hydraulic loaders.

Another unlikely source of trailers was the Ministry of Supply. Lorries and trailers released by the Army, usually described as 'Ex WD', were snapped up for use on farms. Buyers knew that they

Left: Harvested produce in France was often carted direct from the field to a store several kilometres away. As a result French trailer designs had some features that were unusual to British eyes in the mid-1970s. All-welded construction gave great strength with less possibility of leaks. The automatic lifting tailboard saved time and effort when discharging the load, and the sprung drawbar reduced the shock loads imposed on the tractor drawbar. The hydraulic tipping ram was supplied by a PTO-driven pump with its own oil supply. Once French trailers had been seen in Britain, trailer makers found that their customers were asking for the same sort of features in British designs.

Below and Bottom: Specialised trailers are sometimes used to transport potatoes in bulk. To reduce bruising and damage they are carried in a hopper. To empty the trailer a conveyor belt is driven by an electric motor; by controlling the motor speed, the potatoes can be fed straight to a grading line or an elevator. The electrical supply is obtained by plugging the motor into a suitable power socket or extension lead.

had been specified for arduous conditions. Even former bomb trolleys were used on farms.

While all these were eagerly bought for farm use, their design and construction were very different. Each was strongly influenced by what 'the boss' considered an acceptable product to carry his name, and this was reflected in the materials the boss and his employees normally worked with and understood. With material shortages following the war, that had to be tempered by what materials they could obtain. Quite genuinely none of these companies would have contemplated making a trailer the way the others did.

A new type of trailer then started to appear in

Right: Feeding large numbers of cattle is made much easier with a feeder wagon such as this Dutch-built SR. A moving floor brings the load towards the front of the trailer, and revolving beaters tease it out, dropping it on to a fast-moving belt travelling at right angles. This throws out a stream of feed that can be aimed at the troughs. The upper half of the Zetor's cab has been removed to enable it to get into low buildings.

Below right: The rear of a modern tractor, in this case a Massey Ferguson 3070 Autotronic, gives some idea of the various services that can be obtained to power particular implements. The three-point linkage is assisted by two external rams; these raise and lower the link arms, which are fitted with hook catches to engage with heavy implements without manhandling. By using alternative pinholes the driver can determine the amount of rise and fall of the implements. Four outlets can power two separate double-acting rams through the hydraulic service ports; by varying the action of the hydraulic valves they can control a single-acting ram, as here, when the trailer-tipping pipe is plugged in. A separate lower connection is provided for hydraulic trailer braking. This allows the trailer to be braked simultaneously with the tractor foot-brake to permit controlled stopping. Also visible are the electric connections for remote lighting sets.

The power take-off shaft is visible under the guard, which is designed to be tilted up when not required to give a better view of the pick-up hitch. The trailer drawbar is attached to the rear pick-up hitch, which is raised and lowered by the hydraulic linkage. Two tie-rods run from the top of the hydraulic linkage down to the trailer hook. The trailer is fitted with a ring drawbar, which allows the pick-up hook to engage with it to make a positive coupling. When the pick-up hitch is latched in place there is insufficient clearance between the top of the hook and the substantial guard to allow the trailer to become unhitched even if there is no weight on the drawbar.

One fault of drawbar trailers and pick-up hitches still visible in 2000 is the fact that in the event of a tight turn the tractor wheels rub the drawbar. This is a very long-standing problem - similar rubbing could be seen on horse-drawn wagons built over 100 years ago. Some problems take a long time to solve!

response to a demand for cheap trailers that would do just what was claimed for them, designs that were not intended to take severe overloading or abuse. While they proved good value for money, sometimes corners were cut. The standard tyres were very near their capacity, and punctures were rather too common unless the stronger tyre option was specified.

As legally required, brakes were fitted, but the brake shoes were undersized and in some cases the drums were pressed steel. The makers' surprising explanation for this economy was that they were quite adequate if the trailer was stationary before the brakes were applied! Since it was difficult to reach the brake handle from the tractor seat, perhaps they were right! By the late 1970s the police and road safety experts were becoming aware that while tractors could pull these loaded trailers, they had much more difficulty stopping them! Tractors only had brakes on the rear axle, and if the tractor's rear wheels locked with an unbraked trailer there was the risk of the whole outfit skidding into a jack-knife.

As trailers increased in size, tractors were offered with an extra hydraulic tapping that could be used to apply the trailer's brakes simultaneously with the tractor brakes. Tractor gears were permitting faster speeds on the road, even with unsprung tractors, and larger farms spread over a bigger area meant that tractors were travelling further on the road. More comfortable cabs and bigger trailers made it

Top left: When carting loads with a trailer, one of the more irritating jobs is getting off the tractor to release the tailboard to let the load off. This current Richard Western trailer has a hydraulically operated up-and-over rear door, which shaves valuable minutes off the turn-round time, adding up to extra loads over the day. The trailer lights and indicators are well tucked away from risk of damage. A hitch and trailer socket are fitted to allow a second empty trailer to be towed by one tractor when moving from farm to farm.

Below left: Big four-wheel trailers do have disadvantages. They can be difficult to reverse, and most impose very little extra weight on the tractor wheels. In wet conditions that can lead to wheel slip. Charles Marshall of Aberdeenshire offered this long tandem-axle trailer as an alternative. Fitted with tractor-operated brakes and lights, such designs proved popular with farmers fetching baled loads from land away from the main farm.

Bottom: When JCB started to build its prototype High Speed Tractor it was clear that a major job would be transporting loads. Ken Wootton Trailers took up the challenge of building a matching trailer with suspension and full commercial-vehicle-type braking, wheels and tyres. RLM

realistic for farmers to travel further to deliver or fetch produce.

In turn this led to the introduction of the high-speed tractor. For these the legal requirements for trailer braking match those of a commercial vehicle. Trailers are now being supplied with spring suspension and powerful compressed-air-operated brakes.

Trailers used for carting grain from the combine are covered in detail in *An Illustrated History of Combine Harvesters.*

Meanwhile, other engineers were addressing the problem of getting the loads on to the transport. In

Top right and below right: The elevator has always been a useful load-handling implement, and is still ideal for lifting bales up and into awkward-to-reach places. The Lister Anylevel offered plenty of choices to get bales closer to where they were needed. By varying the two ratchet jacks, bales could be carried in through the low doorway or up and over the stored silage as required. A farm conversion has replaced the original wheels with Mini wheels for ease of movement.

the 1940s a few industrial loaders had been built based on agricultural tractors, and were operated by winches and cables; control was by clutching the winch in to raise the load or releasing the winch brake to lower it. These machines were large and clumsy, and were too heavy to risk using on the land.

A few very progressive farmers used small draglines on the farm, converted to hoists to load material, but this was considered most unusual.

Short elevators were offered with a built-in winch so that material could be dragged to the elevator before being lifted and loaded on to carts or trailers. Howard offered its Dungle Dozer, which was a modified Fordson tractor with a powered pick-up reel feeding an elevator. Although a high-output machine, it could only work in well-surfaced yards with ample headroom and manoeuvring space.

The first sign of help for most hard-pressed farm-workers with a fork in their hand was the introduction of the hydraulic system by Ferguson and others. This could operate a buck-rake mounted on a three-point linkage, and for the first time an implement could gather its load, lift it and transport it. Transport boxes could lift a load and transport it even over difficult ground conditions.

Individual manufacturers realised that hydraulic oil could be available under pressure from the tractor, and began to build loading devices of various designs on their tractors. One was mounted

Above right: This flimsy-looking loader was Ferguson's first attempt to mechanise dung handling. Hydraulic rams by the back axle retracted to raise the loader, and it was lowered if the pressure was released. While it may look puny, it could lift the equivalent of a wheelbarrow load, although it made the steering heavy. Here for the first time hydraulic power was doing the lifting rather than a man with a fork.

Right: Ferguson's next design of loader was nicknamed the 'banana loader'. Carefully conceived and profiled, it was expensive to design but economical to make in large numbers. With rams pushing the loader arms up, it had a greater lifting capacity, which meant that it was better able to tear out consolidated dung. The fork was emptied by a push-off blade, which permitted higher discharge. Its main disadvantages were that it made it harder to get on and off the tractor and there was a risk of injury if the driver's arm was on the mudguard when the loader dropped.

Left: The Ferguson earth scoop, already encountered in Chapter 5, could pick up loosened soil and transport it to another nearby unloading spot, and with the weight on the rear wheels it could be used under wet and slippery conditions. Before the availability of bigger machines these were used for many farm construction projects.

Bottom: The American Farmhand loader was one of the strongest normally fitted to British tractors. With a lifting capacity of over 2 tonnes and its own PTO-driven hydraulic pump, it was capable of high and heavy lifts. Unfortunately many of the tractors on which it was originally mounted proved not really strong enough. While this County 7600 Four looks strong enough, the front axle could still become seriously overloaded. In practice a tractor fitted with this big a loader became a dedicated loader tractor and was little used for field work.

on the front axle of a Ferguson tractor; although a relatively small and delicate arrangement, it was able to lift more than a barrow-load at a time. By contrast, more substantial constructions by some manufacturers were so heavy that they spoiled the tractor for any other job except loading.

The hydraulic loader proved a welcome innovation on any farm. Now tractor power could replace manual effort for some shovelling and forking jobs, but not all, because many jobs were still inside awkward buildings or in conditions too slippery for the tractor to get sufficient grip.

Right: American Great Bend loaders were sold by George Brown in Britain. The subframe was designed to fit around the newly introduced safety cab. Again, when used to maximum capacity heavy loads were imposed on the front axle.

Centre left: Even moving relatively small loads can involve hard work if the distance is long or the going hard. A transport box can be lowered to ground level for easy loading, yet when lifted there is ample clearance for travel over rough ground. This Ferguson version was carried on the two lower links with clips to prevent the box from rocking.

Below: Safety cabs offered improved protection for the driver, but initially the combination of a cab and a loader needed some compromises, even when both loader and tractor came from the same manufacturer. On this particular installation part of the front panel has had to be cut away to provide clearance for the control valves and levers to enter the cab. Hydraulic tilt is fitted, allowing the fork to be controlled from the driver's seat; this is helpful when tearing out a load, and gives a more controlled discharge rather that the characteristic all-or-nothing wallop of a trip loader. *RLM*

Top left: The loader subframe on a big tractor like this Nuffield did not obstruct the driver's view too much. However, the front axle and steering used to wear, making steering very imprecise. The trip to release the bucket is by the driver's right elbow.

Below left: The farm lorry had its place in the late 1940s and early 1950s, not only for road haulage but also, in the summer months when the ground was dry enough, for use in the fields. This Commer dates from the late 1940s and is fitted with typical agricultural bodywork. Built up as shown, livestock could be transported to market. Alternatively, the upper three-quarters of the sides could be hinged down and removed. With the upper part of the headboard lifted off and the tailboard removed, the lorry became a dropside for delivering produce, or with all the sides removed it became a platform vehicle for hauling baled forage. While the changes took a bit of work, they allowed more efficient carting, especially if the farm was spread out.

Bottom left: The Cameron Gardner Rearloader (left) fitted on the three-point linkage but had a lift ram as well. Placing extra weight on the rear wheels meant that it could be used in places where a front-loader tractor would get stuck. The rear loader on the right relied purely on the tractor's three-point linkage, so had a more modest capacity. Basic rear loaders of this type were offered by several makers.

Right: Front-end loaders were at a great disadvantage under muddy conditions. Slippery ground reduced the grip of the rear wheels, and the extra weight imposed on the front wheels made them sink in while taking weight off the rear wheels. One answer was the slew loader. The loader arm could swing through 180° and had a reasonable reach from the tractor. With a well-positioned trailer it was often possible to load it without moving tractor or trailer. For a time slew loaders were popular for handling muck and loading sugar beet and lime, but they lost popularity when safety cabs were fitted to tractors and more sophisticated handlers came on the market.

Below right: If the loader arms can be removed when not needed, the tractor is less cluttered. On most early loaders this was quite an involved job and some sort of support had to be improvised, although built-in supports were offered with some. The eventual answer was to combine the supports with a quick-detach arrangement. With practice the loader could be quickly dropped off and parked, leaving the tractor free for other jobs. Grays of Fetterangus made this neatly parked Lynk-on 25 loader. In the foreground is a yard scraper. The warning on the back of the trailer (left) might prevent an impatient motorist mistaking it for a lorry before colliding with it.

Left: Manitou manufactured construction and loading plant in France, and by 1975 its rough-terrain forklifts had the option of four-wheel drive. Pallet forks were still used for many jobs with the options of a dung fork or a bucket.

Below left: Having realised that the loader tractor was doing very little apart from handling, it became obvious that it could be replaced by a purpose-built handler. For this the designer could give priority to getting the design right for handling jobs rather than the compromises of fitting a loader on to an existing tractor. The first innovations came from newcomers rather than established manufacturers. R. W. Collins of Ledbury, Herefordshire, came up with this effective design. The main drive wheels are at the front, and the driver sits up high, enjoying good visibility. At that time most other makers still felt that the future lay in mast-type forklifts.

Most loaders consisted of a substantial subframe bolted permanently to the tractor, to which the loader arms and hydraulic rams were attached by removable pins. With time and trouble they could also be detached. The heavy subframe affected the tractor's usefulness, and as these early loaders were not easy to fit and remove, a converted tractor tended to be regarded as the 'loader tractor'. Popular early attachments were a dung fork or a bucket; less common were a crane hook or a dozer blade.

Discharging was usually accomplished by pulling a trip lever, which released a catch allowing the attachment to tip forward, instantly dumping the whole load. In theory, once emptied it would rebound and latch itself again. With a sloppy bucketful, a mess would result if the trip was released with the bucket too high! Sometimes the catch would release accidentally, hence frequent safety warnings about not standing in the bucket.

Up to the early 1950s tractors had hydraulic pumps that stopped working when the clutch was depressed. To raise the loader it was necessary to select neutral and lift the clutch pedal. With hindsight this was a nuisance, but at the time was quite acceptable and one of only a few minor drawbacks. A loader represented the first mechanical means of picking up a load from ground level and getting it on to a trailer or other means of transport, and was a great boon on the farm for most jobs. However, it did little to make the tractor driver's job easier. Before power steering, manoeuvring the tractor meant hard and continuous effort to do the work of three or four people with hand tools.

Tractor loader design continued to evolve, and H. Cameron Gardner Ltd pioneered the concept of mounting a loading arrangement on the rear three-point linkage of the tractor. Whereas a conventional

Right: Here was a tool that could lift and transport considerable loads over difficult ground conditions while the operator was out of the weather and enjoying light power steering. The front wheels of a conventional loader would have sunk badly in wet conditions like these, making movement very difficult.

Below: This 16-year-old Teleshift, which had lost all its cab glazing and with bald tyres, still attracted keen bidding when auctioned off as part of a retirement sale. Both the fork and bucket are fitted with quick-attach mountings.

loader removed weight from the back wheels, encouraging wheel spin, the extra weight of the rear loader and load went mainly on to the driving wheels, giving more grip.

The idea of a loader that could be quickly detached and parked was pioneered by a Scandinavian manufacturer and marketed in the UK as the 'Quickie Loader'. Careful design and the use of high-tensile steel meant that subframe brackets were becoming lighter. This, together with the ability to drop the loader off quickly, meant that the tractor was almost unencumbered for other jobs.

Industrial users wanted even greater strength, and soon more specialised loaders were meeting this need. Tractor manufacturers started to offer an industrial loader version of a popular model of agricultural tractor, but underneath it was still a recognisable tractor skid unit. Later in their lives some of these specialised industrial machines finished their existence working in agriculture. Farmers have always had an eye for a bargain, and some surprising machines still finish up on farms once they have become cheap enough to acquire.

For some industrial-type applications a forklift-type mast took less space, typical jobs being picking up pallets and box crates. A typical early on-the-farm modification, where a forklift mast was grafted on to a Ferguson 35 tractor, is illustrated in *An Illustrated History of Tractors*. Various manufacturers took up this idea, and soon a range of forklift masts was available. Most fitted on the rear three-point linkage, but some attached to the front end of the tractor instead. While they were useful, early forklifts had a number of

Above: The design was later acquired by Matbro of Tetbury, Gloucestershire. While cosmetic improvements were made, Matbro initially retained the basic design. Entrance to the cab was by the steps at the rear, and the hitch was to tow a trailer. A later design of Matbro handler is pictured in *An Illustrated History of Forklift Trucks*.

Below: A telescopic loader has done much to ease handling jobs around the farm. With this flat-eight bale grab it can pick up eight bales and stack them either on a trailer or in a stack; indeed, the bales can be untouched by hand until required for use in the winter. Another whole series of hot and tiring jobs has been eliminated by one versatile machine. One hazard is that thoughtless use of the lift and boom extension could easily bring down the telephone cable; were it to be a high-voltage electricity cable, you have yet another way of killing or injuring yourself on the farm.

disadvantages. With the forks down the mast was often substantially higher that the load, and while the load would pass under an overhead obstruction, the top of the mast might clout it vigorously!

Some farmers found it worth while to mount buckets or forks on to tractor-mounted forklifts, finding that the forklift was more compact to use than a conventional tractor and loader. Since a rear-mounted forklift usually needed extra ballast on the front end of the tractor to hold the nose down, a few farmers specified a forklift on the rear and a loader on the front to produce a specialised handling tractor. While these were awkward lumps, they were able to tackle the jobs that cropped up on most farms.

One of the early pioneers of tractor-mounted forklifts was Sanderson of Croft, near Skegness. Mr Sanderson Senior had been a very successful wheelwright in the area, and he and his son Roy were early pioneers of linkage-mounted forklifts. They then started modifying tractors, reversing their operation. This brought the forklift mast to the front of a machine with rear-wheel steering. The remainder of the story can be found in *An Illustrated History of Forklift Trucks*, pp92-99.

In the Loire in France, Braud was mounting forklift masts on the back of modified French-built

Above: The chassis of a handler is a compromise between two desirable features: the shorter the wheelbase the more manoeuvrable the machine becomes, while a longer wheelbase gives stability and reduces any tendency to tip forward. Sanderson found a good compromise with four-wheel steering; now even a long-wheelbase machine became manoeuvrable. *RLM*

Inset left: Sambron was another French pioneer and was quick to adopt hydrostatic transmission. For the first Tractor Pull at the Royal Show in 1978 a demonstrator was used to level the track. When the crowds had dispersed, for a laugh, it was hitched to the sledge. Ballasted with a full bucket it made a 'full pull'. What impressed those that had stayed to mock was that there was no wheel slip, nor did the engine labour. It may have been slow and unspectacular, but to technical observers it was an impressive demonstration of future trends in handler design.

Below: Kramer was a German tractor-maker before specialising in compact four-wheel-drive loaders. This Allrad loader has been used to load powdered lime into the spreader normally towed by the JCB Fastrac. This one-man outfit is hitching up ready to move to another job in North Yorkshire.

Left: Manitou has come a long way since it first hung a forklift mast on an old International Pony tractor. All the components, with the firm's carefully profiled designs, show an investment in design. With a large push-off buckrake it is well suited to moving and placing large quantities of grass, as seen at this demonstration of silage-making.

Below left: At the same event New Holland demonstrated its Canadian built bi-directional tractor. In this pivot-steer vehicle, the operator and the main controls can face in either direction as required.

Below: MFT Ireland was the home of the Moffett MFT, a cross between a handler and a tractor. Based on a Ford skid unit, it too was bi-directional and capable of field work. *RLM*

Far right: A skid-steer loader needs no conventional steering system. Instead, by varying the speed and rotation of the two pairs of wheels it can be manoeuvred even in a confined space. Here the demonstrator felt that the audience would appreciate a chance to inspect his machine from an unusual angle.

Right: For some jobs a loader that bends in the middle is preferred. Turning the steering wheel of a pivot-steer machine allows the whole boom to swing over an arc even when stationary. Attachments can be quickly changed to suit the current job. Here the demonstrator is simulating putting a bale into a pen from a narrow passage as part of a JCB display.

International Cub tractors These became specialised self-propelled forklifts, known as Manitous. It was 10 years before they were first exported to Britain.

Other manufacturers such as Sambron took up this idea of self-propelled rough-terrain forklift trucks. Again, commercial examples of various makes on building sites can be seen in *An Illustrated History of Forklift Trucks*. As with self-propelled sprayers, more sophisticated and elaborate designs emerged from various workshops. Manufacturers ceased to make use of tractor skid units and built dedicated machines for the job.

Recognising the limitations of a vertical forklift mast, there was a general move towards using hydraulic rams and a boom to take the attachment. With some designs the boom was made telescopic and could extend as well, which meant that the same loader could have either a good lifting capacity or increased lifting height. Extra traction could be obtained by offering four-wheel drive, and manoeuvrability could be improved by making the loader 'bend in the middle' with articulated steering. Other makers used some form of electronic control allowing either front or rear wheels to steer or, with both axles steering, to travel crabwise or at an angle. Conventional loaders were being mounted on four-wheel-drive tractors for increased grip and output.

Most manufacturers offer a quick-change feature so that attachments can be more easily exchanged, and the range of attachments has grown. While the fork and bucket are still widely used, they have been joined by the bale-handler, the livestock feeder, pallet forks, the rotary brush and the personnel lift for access to high locations, as well as more specialised equipment to take advantage of the handler's power and lifting capacity. Every extra complication added was intended to allow a skilled operator to work faster and get more work done.

The handler seen on many farms today is far removed from a tractor fitted with an attachment. Even farms that cannot justify a brand-new machine are eager customers for a second-hand one. Handlers now are dedicated special-purpose machines, and while they are still mounted on tractor-type tyres, emphasis has been given to traction and rough-terrain ability as well as stability with big loads. Drivers have fully power-operated steering and in some cases air-conditioning. It is a tribute to the versatile nature of handlers that new owners have always reported that they are being used far more than predicted each year.

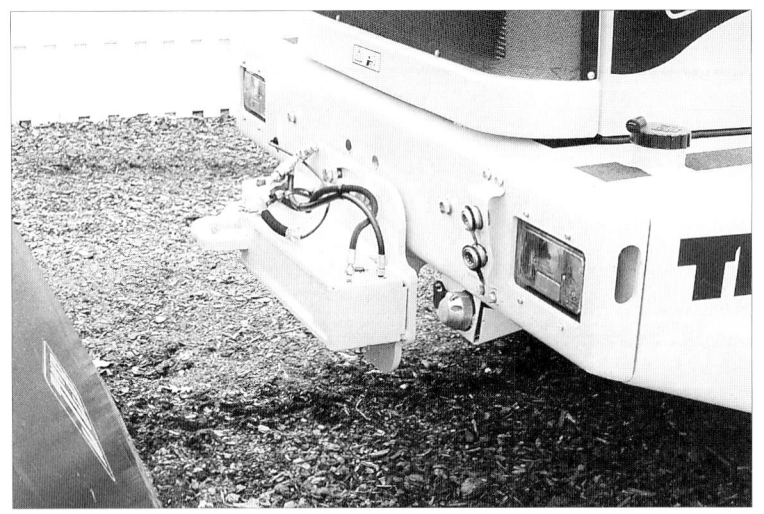

Left: An important part of the sales effort of a major manufacturer nowadays is to make users dissatisfied with their existing machine. One very effective way to do this is with a slick demonstration of the virtues of the latest machine, and JCB have always had a reputation for the professionalism of their demonstrators. With space at a premium, they manage with what seems an extremely small and cramped demonstration area, and by careful planning they are still able to demonstrate the features of several machines. Tricks like standing a Loadall on its nose at the Royal Show in 2000 illustrate what a skilled operator can do. The greased part of the boom can be extended or retracted as required. The archway was to demonstrate how low a building it could enter.

Left: JCB offer a pick-up hitch for towing a trailer, which is arranged so that it can be swung to one side if it would dig in or catch on obstructions.

Bottom left: Many of those watching appear only casually interested, but shrewd sales people know that serious customers like to mingle with the crowd to make their first assessment of a new machine. For 2000 one machine featured on the JCB stand at the Royal Show was this 520-50. The watching crowd was particularly impressed with how quickly and easily the driver could change the attachments on the machine. So the process continues of farmers looking for more up-to-date implements to make their farming more productive as they carry on producing food to feed a hungry world.

Epilogue

With all this talk of implements, arable farming seems a very mechanical process. Certainly most successful arable farmers have a knack of getting the best out of machinery.

Just take a moment to wonder at the scale of a farmer's achievements. He prepares soil to a condition where it is likely to grow a useful crop. Some form of expensive seed is planted and tended. If all goes well this seed grows. How well it grows will depend on the weather conditions - whether it rains enough or too much. Will the farmer respond in time and successfully to threats to the crop from weeds, fungus, diseases, slugs, aphids and other pests? Other threats can come from rabbits chewing off the crop when young, straying livestock, or even fire in some crops just before harvest. Most crops have diseases to which they are particularly prone. Even when the crop is ready, hail can damage it or flooding can make the ground too wet for harvesting, while early frost can affect crops that are normally harvested late in the year. If all goes well - and it is a big 'if' - the farmer hopes to harvest enough from the fields to be able to feed you and the rest of the non-farming world.

All these stages have cost money, and the farmer alone has carried the risk. Only after the crop is harvested safely can the farmer hope for any return for his effort. To a farmer a successful harvest is a combination of yield and the price that he gets for the crop, which he hopes will provide enough money for him to do it again next year. After meeting these costs he will still have to pay interest or rent on the cost of the land. His constant hope is that there will be enough left over to provide an income to live on and maybe some money to invest in improvements to the farm, including perhaps replacing an implement.

Over the last few years falling prices have meant that many farmers are in the extraordinary position that they are having to take jobs off the farm to make it possible to carry on farming. One could understand this if there really were massive food surpluses, as politicians would have us believe. Yet the true picture with grain, for example, is very different. Bearing in mind that it takes a year to grow a crop, you would expect the world to carry pretty substantial reserves against the risk of crop failures, but spread over the whole world we have a reserve of less than 10 weeks' consumption. It makes you realise just how vital a job our farmers are doing.

If you want to see implements at work there are a number of possibilities. If you live in the country you may see them at work in local fields. Depending on the farmer, they might be old implements still doing a useful job, or modern equipment making a fleeting visit. It is always claimed that farmers are bad drivers because they are 'farming over the hedge'. Don't fall into the same trap, but as a passenger you are likely to spot some machinery at work in the course of a journey.

'Steam Rally', 'Vintage Gathering', 'Vintage Working', 'Ploughing Match', 'Technical Demonstration' - the name will vary, but typically these pleasant rural events are held on farmland and are likely to include tractors, steam engines, horses, and perhaps an area of ground where some of the implements can work. Some specialist museums have a strong rural bias featuring implements as part of rural history. If you are in an unfamiliar part of the country, or even abroad, try the local tourist office for suggestions. Leave your enquiry open-ended and you might be delighted with their suggestions.

There are a number of locally-based clubs around the country that cater for steam or tractor enthusiasts, and this is where you are likely to find implement collectors congregating. The biggest of these is the National Vintage Tractor and Engine Club, which has about 30 locally-based groups with a substantial number of affiliated local clubs. To find your nearest club, ring 01454 321010 (in the UK).

A final word on safety. Most of the implements described in this book are deliberately built very ruggedly. If you come into accidental contact with an implement in use, be in no doubt that you will come off worse, either badly injured or even killed.

The size of modern implements and tractors means that they have blind spots. Many power-driven implements can hurl stones or other missiles with surprising force. As we have seen, they can require a surprising amount of space when turning. Even experienced farmers and farm workers get caught out and killed each year by machinery.

For your own safety, give machinery a wide berth. Always assume that the driver or operator has not seen you. Probably the safest place to see agricultural machinery is at one of the larger agricultural shows, where it is on static display and sometimes demonstrated as well.

The most sobering thought is that all this machinery is manufactured for one purpose only - to ensure that you and your fellow human beings need never go hungry again.

Below: The tractor seat is a good place to study the causes of crop losses. These could include a wet spot, excessive weeds, or pest damage, but the problem here is the local council, which has rediscovered a long-forgotten footpath. The resulting damage has been caused by efforts to keep it clear for hikers, and revealingly, although the crop has been cut back, there has not been enough foot traffic to control the weeds that have flourished in its place.